CAUGHT!
Prisoner-of-War no.487

The author at 163rd Officer Cadet Training Unit, Folkestone, November 1939.

CAUGHT!
Prisoner-of-War no.487

DORRIEN BELSON

Dorrien Belson
29th May 2003

Bentwyck Henry Publishers Ltd

Published by: Bentwyck Henry Publishers Ltd
36 Hart Street
Henley-on-Thames
Oxfordshire, RG9 2AU, England
National: 01491 413100
International: (+44) 1491 413100
Email: bentwyckhenrybks@aol.com
Website: www.bentwyckhenry-publishers.com

Cover design by DNA Design Consultants

Typeset in Monotype Baskerville by
John Saunders Design & Production, Southmoor OX13 5HU

Printed and Bound in Great Britain by
Antony Rowe Ltd, Bumper's Farm Industrial Estate
Chippenham, Wiltshire SN14 6LH

Jacket and colour insert printed by Raven Print (Oxon) Ltd.
Unit B13, Borough Road, Buckingham Road Industrial Estate
Brackley, Northants NN13 7BE

Foreword

It is indeed a great pleasure and privilage to write a few words in support of Dorrien Belson's memoir of his years spent in Prisoner of War camps during the Second World War.

I have known Dorrien since about 1943, when we were Prisoners of War together in Germany. Never having met prior to to this date we were thrown together by the fortunes of war. Since then, however, we have become the best of friends.

Having read this book I can confirm that it gives a very accurate description of everyday life in a Prisoner of War camp in the Third Reich – from the sometimes horrific to the occasionally humorous conditions and situations we found ourselves in.

I wish this book every success.

Philip Varley, 2003

To my sons,
Roger, Timothy and John Anthony,
and daughter Lucy
with love.

Contents

List of Illustrations

Acknowledgements

I am much indebted to my wife, Mary, for her continual encouragement and help; to the late Duke of Norfolk, who urged me to seek publication, and to Mary Selwyn, who did likewise, and followed this up with much practical assistance and advice. I am also most grateful to Philip Varley for his helpful comments and for allowing me to include a specially interesting anecdote involving him personally. Also to Major (Retired) CPT Rebbeck, The Archivist for the Royal Gloucestershire, Berkshire and Wiltshire Regiment and for the Soldiers of Gloucestershire Museum, for his assistance with regimental records. My thanks are also due to others who have helped in various ways, including Gerry Hall and Toby Greenwood.

Thanks to The National Army Museum, London for permission to reproduce the bust of my ancestor Gen. Sir Charles Phillip Benson.

Every effort has been made to trace the copyright holders of illustrations. The publisher would be grateful for any information regarding their identity.

Preface

All the privations of life as a prisoner-of-war – the loss of freedom, the constant subjection to an enemy control, the occasional very real hunger and the many long periods of biting cold – are as nothing when compared with the truly appalling horrors and atrocities that befell so many hundreds of thousands of people in Europe and Japan during the Second World War. It is salutary to bear such things in mind, and it helps to maintain a sense of proportion, so essential when writing about oneself.

In this attempt at a brief war autobiography, in endeavouring to present an overall impression of events that actually took place some sixty years ago, my memory has been jolted into action. The process has been somewhat akin to disturbing a bottle of vintage wine that has lain peacefully in dark cellars for many years. As the bottle is held up to the glare of unaccustomed light, particles of sediment can be seen floating around. I have tried to sift what I can but some of them have already sunk to the depths from which they arose and are probably best left there.

In his book '*The Egoist*', George Meredith wrote: '...cellars... are... cloisters where the bottle meditates on joys to bestow...' This particular bottle may not generate much joy, but, with all its omissions and no doubt some errors too, I hope it will go some way to satisfying whatever curiosity may have been aroused.

Dorrien Belson
November, 2003

THE PRISONERS

Dulce et Decorum est pro Patria Mori

We whom no bullet found nor gave
The honour of an early grave;
O'er whom no oratory shall roll
Its pomp of phrase to crush the soul;
Who, through no fault of ours, alive
Gave but four years of youth, or five,
So that no epitaph proclaims
Our names among those other "names
That live for evermore" (so runs
The standard fame conferred by guns)
We did not die in vain – ah, no.
We live in vain – and better so.
We from the dead shall rise again
And certain things for them explain;
How death in battle often seems
Most rudely heckled by men's screams;
How dead men yet demand our skill
To lift them up – lest they should spill;
How sometimes one of them will stir,
With "Put me out, for Christ's sake, Sir."
But shall we stop the mouths of fools
For future wars concocting rules?
Or will our memory disdain
To speak, until war comes again?
Shall we whom men so soon forgot
Pretend that all the dead are not?
Or shall we, hearing men declare
That death in battle is most fair,
Recall how once our youth was spent,
Wonder, - and silently assent?
This sweet and splendid thing, to die –
Why did such glory pass us by?

E.J.M. Buxton, 1945

Introduction

Fathers of my generation are apt to be asked what they did in the war. The question arises not so much from the curiosity of children as from young adults, whose deeper interest merits an openhearted reply. Those fathers with a distinguished war record would probably find little difficulty in responding, other than coping with certain modesty about their achievements. I should have liked to have been one of them, but I have a very different story to relate and one I have made no previous attempts to write. I only do so now because I have been encouraged to and because I have been led to believe that it might be of interest to others beyond my immediate family.

Strange at it may seem, my war years have never been the subject – apart from an isolated anecdote – of any letter or conversation that I can recall having had with anyone at any time, even closest family. Although there are valid reasons for this, which are explained later on, it remains a curious fact that what appear to be momentous events in one's life can, nevertheless, be passed by without any reference being made to them, much less any discussion about them. In wartime this is hardly surprising because so many others would be in the throes of so many more varied and exciting experiences, and, so many stories having already been related, who indeed would want to hear any more? This, then, is written more to a younger generation who have not had first-hand experience of warfare. In no way is it a war history; it is solely an impression of what happened to, and how it affected, just one person.

The history of our family service in both the Army and the Royal Navy since the middle of the eighteenth century has been well recorded. Most of it can be seen in the National Army Museum in London, where the bust of our ancestor General Sir Charles Philip Belson is displayed together with his Peninsular Gold Cross with four clasps. His other medals and those of his nephew General George John Belson, who fought with him in the Peninsular War, are also displayed. Sir Philip went on to serve under Wellington in 1815 and commanded the 28th of Foot – The Gloucestershire Regiment – at the battle of Waterloo.

Bust of Gen. Sir Charles Philip Belson, KCB, KH, courtesy of The National Army Museum.

General Sir Horace Smith-Dorrien, GCB, GCMG, DSO, Godfather to the author.

This tradition of military service no doubt prompted my parents, in the midst of the First World War, to name me, like my brother Philip, after some equally notable military figure. At the beginning of that war, the two Corps Commanders were General Haig and General Sir Horace Smith-Dorrien. The latter was well known to my grandparents, and shortly after my birth in February 1917 he consented to be my Godfather, and this is how I came to bear my name.

With all this auspicious background of military distinction, my young might well have imagined that their father would have risen effortlessly to the rank of Field Marshal. Sadly for them, and I suppose even more so for me, this is not a story of any greatness nor of a conquering hero proudly returning home from overseas covered in glory, but of one who was involved in the devastating defeat of the British Expeditionary Force to France in 1940, with the added humiliation of almost five years as a prisoner-of-war. Close association for so long with such experiences does not tend to inspire bright conversation about them, so the lack of communication all this time is perhaps not so strange after all.

I am only too aware that very many others, whether in the Services or as civilians, were subjected to far worse experiences than ever came my way. Even now, in peacetime, terrible things can happen. For instance, each of my grown-up children could relate some such story; whether it be the consequences of a serious road accident; soldiering amidst the troubles in Northern Ireland; suffering physical handicap from birth; or the traumas of working for a lengthy period in an Intensive Care Unit in a hospital.

The poem on page xii, 'The Prisoners, *Dulce et Decorum est pro Patria Mori*' was written by John Buxton in February, 1945, after nearly five years in German and Polish prisoner-of-war camps. He was clearly influenced by a quotation from Horace (65–8 BC) – "It is a sweet and splendid thing to die for your fatherland." Buxton couldn't stomach the sheer stupidity, as he saw it, of those who would glorify war. Although tinged with bitterness, which I did not share, his poem was very well received, and I am indebted to his memory for being able to reproduce it.

PART ONE

The Advent of War

"Now tell us about the war,
and what they fought each other for."

Robert Southey, 1774–1843

AT 11.15 am on 3rd September, 1939, The Prime Minister – Neville Chamberlain – announced on the radio that Great Britain was at war with Nazi Germany. The previous day, in the House of Commons, Chamberlain had still held out the prospect of "Peace for our time", and had given no clear statement that any ultimatum had been sent to Germany, nor that a second one would be sent at 9.00 am on 3rd September. Both of the British Government's ultimatums were ignored, and so now we were at war.

Within half-an-hour wailing sirens were giving Londoners their first air-raid warning. At home with my parents in their flat near Roehampton, I joined them as we all dutifully responded by assembling in the air-raid shelter, which was in the garden and immediately under a bed of roses. "How convenient," my mother observed, "If we get hit here we shall be in our ready-made grave complete with flowers above – no need for wreaths." This was the first and only time I can remember ever being in an air-raid shelter.

To a 22-year-old, as I then was, the thought of war was exciting, adventurous, and glamorous even, with all sorts of exhilarating opportunities to join with others in fighting for one's country. To my parents, however, who had already learnt what war was really like, it was horrifying, devastating and utterly tragic. The First World War, which was 'to end all wars', had itself ended only just over twenty years earlier. It was almost unbelievable to them that they should now be on the verge of having to experience another war, and this time with three sons of military age.

I don't think either I or any of my contemporaries thought very deeply about why we were being called upon to fight, and apart from a few conscientious objectors no-one queried the rights or wrongs of doing so. It seemed clear enough that some attempts had to be made to curb the aggression of a dominating Dictator, and that was enough. A call to arms by one's country was all that was needed to arouse an immediate response.

The build-up to war

For the Germans the same patriotic call to arms brought the same response, but the purpose for it was entirely different. Under the

Nazi regime, Germany had been steadily and quite openly preparing for war, certainly since 1936. In that year they had begun their persecution of the Jews; first by humiliating them and then by ridding the country of anyone who had any trace of Jewish blood. This was accomplished in a most brutal manner and although it brought protests from various parts of the civilised world no country took any positive action to stop it. Hitler's repeated demands for more 'Lebensraum' – living space – for Germany's expanding population led to the successive occupation of the Rhineland, Sudetanland, Austria and Czechoslovakia. He then turned his attention to Poland, demanding a corridor to the Baltic port of Danzig, and threatened invasion of that country if his demands were opposed. This marked the turning point, which finally convinced the British Government that it was imperative to take action to check any further aggression, and which, in turn, led to the declaration of war.

By 1939, Hitler's power was almost absolute. He was a forceful leader who had succeeded in mesmerising the nation into believing that now they had their opportunity to expunge the humiliation of their Great War defeat in 1918. Any scruples that any of them may have had about their war being right or wrong would have been easily overridden by the obvious power Germany was now enjoying, which had already brought them outstanding successes in the ruthless expansion of their own territory. Such was the might of the Nazi regime that any dissident would have been, and in fact was, destined for a very short life.

As were to learn only too clearly a few months later, Britain was not at all ready for a land war, more especially against a massive well-trained German army. It seems incredible that such an appalling lack of preparation should have stemmed from the belief held by leading politicians and other influential persons that whatever the apparent danger, somehow actual war would be averted. Maybe there were a number of politicians who did believe that war could not be avoided, yet shrank from expressing their views publicly for fear of courting unpopularity. These leaders of our nation were somehow snared by wishful thinking, or just blind optimism, and the effect of their inaction at a time of mounting crisis was largely responsible for the early military disasters and reverses suffered in 1940. Amongst the very few who spoke out in the spring and summer of 1939, maintaining that war was not just inevitable but would come very soon, was Winston Churchill, but he and those who were in accord with his view were ridiculed. Consequently, even during the approach to the autumn of 1939, life went on much as usual.

The German ambassador to Britain, von Ribbentrop, who was hanged as a war criminal after the war, could be seen circulating amidst the social life of London exuding an atmosphere of calm and peace whilst his countrymen were intensifying their preparations to attack us. On one occasion, however, which was widely reported, he caused a stir at a formal function by raising his right arm in the new Nazi salute. This was deemed to be a serious *faux pas* and earned him the nickname 'Brickendrop'.

Even King George VI was convinced that war could still be averted by negotiation. He wrote as much to Ena, the exiled English Queen of Spain, in a letter dated 27th August 1939 – just seven days before war was declared.

To make matters even worse, our politicians, newspapers and radio programmes had for months been pouring out the sort of propaganda that would have us believe that the enemy were almost starving and on the verge of revolution; that they were ill-equipped and lacked the resources to maintain even what they had. In one memorable article it was claimed that hundreds of German tanks were made of plywood, and were merged in with real ones to create the impression of greater strength. The one I was to see at close range in France a few months later was very solid and bristled with armour.

Training

Soon after leaving school in 1934, aged 17, I had followed my elder brother into the Territorial Army. We both served in a London Anti-Aircraft Unit, which sported one gun only with the date 1912 stamped on it. It had a range, we were told, of nearly 10,000 feet. The technology of the day also provided us with a 'Predictor'. Into this magic box we had to record the estimated speed and direction of the enemy plane, point it to where we thought the plane might be and then, following its calculations, fire the gun in the fervent hope that our target wasn't flying too fast or too high.

I had by then found employment with a well-known company of wine merchants, and was required by them to move to Bristol for at least a year to undergo instruction in the handling of wine. This took place in their cellars every morning and was followed by further instructions each afternoon on the appreciation of wine itself. All this involved a considerable amount of tasting. Each day I was to face rows of glasses of sherry, port, or red and white table wines, and had to learn about each one, record copious notes and commit the varying nuances in colour, bouquet and taste to memory. Tasters are obliged, for obvious reasons, not to swallow what they taste but can never completely avoid some wine slipping down the gullet. After a full day's work my main concern was how quickly I could get back to my digs and lie down for a while – and on one occasion how to stop the room going round. It was therefore with great relief that I soon discovered there was no local Anti-Aircraft Unit to which I could transfer, and to which I might otherwise be expected to report after a day in the heady alcohol-laden atmosphere of the ancient cellars which were my new workplace.

I had accordingly to resign from the Territorial Army, but on my return to London in 1938, and being rather disillusioned with the prospects in Anti-Aircraft defence, I joined an infantry Unit – The Artists Rifles – one of the City of London Regiments. Before the war, annual holidays rarely exceeded three weeks. One of the advantages of signing on in the TA was that an extra week's holiday would usually be granted provided two weeks were spent at a TA summer camp. It is my recollection that these annual camps, though under military discipline and therefore taken fairly seriously, were on the whole reasonably good fun spent in the company of a number of like-minded friends. Whilst reaping benefits from all the training, we were happy in the knowledge that we were doing something worthwhile for ourselves as well as something, however small, for our country.

The annual camp in August 1939 at Warminster, however, was not much fun at all. Apart from being flooded out of our tents for much of the time with incessant rain, the whole fortnight was treated very seriously by the Commanding Officer, who was obviously one of those who believed that war was imminent. We were all made to realise the seriousness of proper training and as it turned out were very glad to have had this brief opportunity to experience virtual war conditions, especially as war was declared just less than three weeks later.

Two weeks after war was declared, I was posted to 163 Officer Cadet Training Unit at Shorncliffe Barracks near Folkestone, where I was to undergo three months of intensive training in order to qualify for a commission. The course had been carefully crafted to ensure that the maximum effort would be extracted from all cadets, both physically and mentally. It was made clear from the outset that if we aspired to the rank of officer, we would be expected to be capable of doing anything that we might order anyone under our command to do; and furthermore we should be able to do it even more efficiently. There was little time set aside for any relaxation, and no leave apart from one weekend in the middle of the course. Every hour of every day was filled with some activity or other and some of the nights too were devoted to training in the dark. Whatever the day held for us we were always highly relieved when it was finally time for bed. The beds were, unfortunately, not very comfortable, that is for anyone of the normal height of 6 feet or more, because the dormitories we were in had previously been used by a boarding school for rather small children.

At regular intervals we would be given progress tests, each of which had to be passed successfully. There was what is now called zero tolerance, and the very few who failed any test were obliged to pack up and leave. Time at Shorncliffe seemed to pass with incredible speed and before we realised it we were into the last week of the course and heading for the all-important final examinations, both practical and written.

The time already spent in the Territorial Army proved to be of immense value in enabling me to pass out successfully with the result that I was granted the rank of Second Lieutenant just before Christmas 1939. At that time even a single pip on one's shoulder was a matter of modest pride, conferring as it did on its wearer a degree, however limited, of authority and command. This was something real, especially in time of war. It was exciting, and, although a Second-Lieutenant was still the lowest commissioned rank in the army, it was probably the first experience any of us had had of actual responsibility on which others could be dependent, possibly even for their lives – a very sobering thought that rightly tempered any exaggerated feelings of self-importance.

All of us were given the opportunity of indicating which regiment we should like to join without any guarantee being offered that our wishes would be met. Most preferences were in fact respected, apart from one misguided officer who wrote that he would be happy to join any regiment except one in particular which he named. In accordance with the long-standing traditions of the army, he was, of course, posted to that regiment. For family historical reasons I elected to join the Gloucestershire Regiment and was instructed to report to their Headquarter Company early in January, 1940, at Horfield Barracks in Bristol.

I had already visited Horfield Prison, as it was previously, only a year or so before. In 1938 the Prison Governor had invited my employers to send someone to talk to the inmates about wine. Inexperienced as I was in the world of wine – and maybe because of this – I was told to give the talk. On arrival at the prison, I was, rather surprisingly, conducted to the Chapel, where some forty inmates were already assembled, and was asked to mount the steps of the pulpit. My growing misgivings about having been mistaken for some visiting missionary must have been apparent to the Prison Officer, who quickly reassured me by explaining that all 'entertainment', as he put it, came from the pulpit. My immediate thoughts about what sort of entertainment anyone else might have provided in this unlikely setting were quickly dismissed as I surveyed my captive audience.

My first impression was that most, if not all, of them had turned up out of curiosity, and I sensed a total lack of vibes, which was hardly surprising. Undeterred, I launched into the subject, but it soon occurred to me that one particular aspect might be of a more practical interest to them – those wines, like vintage port, which needed several years to mature before being ready to drink. However, in the event it seemed insensitive to mention any specific number of years, and so after rambling on for nearly half an hour it was time for questions. A lag at the back – why, I wondered do all awkward questions come from the back? – asked me if I would explain how to make hooch. Thankfully, there was no time to reply as the presiding Prison Officer had suddenly leapt to his feet and was sternly announcing that the talk was now over.

The austere surroundings of Horfield Barracks now formed the background for the Headquarter Company which I had just joined, and where I was to find that the army at that time was still very formal. It didn't take very long to learn that in the Officer's Mess the three subjects, apart from 'shop', that must never be raised were religion, politics and women. Junior officers hardly uttered unless they were spoken to first – a rare occurrence. In that very cold winter, life anyway for a brief spell was not all that uncomfortable. I had a room to myself with an open coal fire, which was attended to by a batman, who also coped with all the spit and polish so dear to the hearts of generations of commanding officers. This period of formal indoctrination ended after three weeks and I was not sorry to be transferred to the highly relaxed atmosphere of the Junior Officer's Mess, where life was distinctly different. There appeared to be no restrictions on conversation in this Mess and as we were all much the same age the sort of topics that most of us were or could be interested in were given full range of expression.

At the Holding Unit

Few of us were properly fitted out, and we began to wonder when we would be issued with the three pieces of equipment all officers were supposed to possess – a pistol, a compass and a pair of binoculars. In spite of these deficiencies I was allotted a platoon of 28 men, most of whom were quite a bit older than myself. Almost three months of small-arms training, square bashing and parades of all kinds, including Church Parades, which at that time were still compulsory, suddenly ended when several of us received orders to transfer to a Holding Unit at Ludlow in Shropshire, where we were confidently assured, all our missing equipment would be provided.

A Holding Unit was an interim depot where troops were assembled for final training before being sent to a war zone. On arrival at Ludlow our group of five officers duly reported at the destination we had been given only to find absolutely nothing there at all. It was completely empty – not even a pen or any paper. After visiting the men who had preceded us and who were billeted not far away, we set about providing ourselves with one of the essential trappings of authority by equipping a makeshift headquarters. We thought this was our major problem but were to learn of a much more pressing one almost immediately.

The men, having had very little to do and as yet not being much organised, had resorted to the local pubs where they were quickly introduced to the local speciality – cider. This innocent looking drink, which some of them were led to believe to be virtually non-alcoholic, was rough, very potent and went by the highly appropriate name of 'Stunnem Tanglefoot'. A pint or two was enough to make the drinker glow with the feeling that all was well with the world in the warm atmosphere of the bar, but, unaccountably, on emerging into the cold night air his legs suddenly became like jelly and he would collapse on the ground wondering what on earth had hit him. Pubs had to be put out of bounds and the men found something to do, and as I remember it we hurriedly began to get them, and indeed ourselves, properly organised.

Training: Officer Cadets at the Holding Unit. Dorrien Belson: front row, 4th from the left.

At this early stage in the war there was a shortage of equipment for the men and even more so for the officers. We presumed that many of the items we needed would be on their way to us soon, and meanwhile we were to fend for ourselves as best we could. This entailed holding parades, arranging route marches, giving talks – all routine procedure and deadly dull until one bright day a big box arrived out of the blue. This turned out to be a new weapon known as the Boyes anti-tank rifle. Its name was hardly reassuring, and we wondered if it had been intended for us anyway; we couldn't have requested it, not even knowing of its existence. However, having received it, we read the instructions and, to liven up the day, decided to test it.

The weapon was designed to be fired from the shoulder and, having a bullet considerably larger than that of a standard rifle, it would penetrate the armour of a tank and then ricochet around inside causing havoc and panic amongst the crew. I had noticed in the manual, in rather small print, that there was likely to be a substantial kick. I fervently hoped therefore that someone else would volunteer to be the first to fire it. No such luck! Others, it appeared, had also scanned the small print. It was agreed that we should draw lots to decide who should have the honour of being the first to fire it. It's always been difficult to understand why success has hardly ever come my way in lotteries, draws or even raffles, yet in such situations as I was now faced with I would have no problem in 'winning', which is exactly what happened. Assuming an air of totally misplaced confidence, I loaded the weapon with what seemed to be a mini-shell, held it to my shoulder, aimed at a distant target and pulled the trigger. I was immediately thrown to the ground as though kicked by a mule. Scrambling to my feet and observing my fellow officers standing around apparently awe-struck, I suggested somewhat coldly that one of them might like to have a go. There was, however, a sudden drop in enthusiasm for the new weapon and one or two, glancing at their watches, suddenly remembered other pressing duties, and so it was hurriedly agreed that the new weapon should be set aside for further practice at some later date. The only time I ever saw it used again in England was as punishment for any soldier convicted of some misdemeanour, who was ordered to fire it.

Although war had been declared over seven months earlier very little action had yet taken place. This period of comparative calm came to be known as the Phoney War. There were still a number of politicians and other leaders of public opinion who seriously believed that even at this late stage actual fighting could still be averted. The worst part of this prolonged lull was the continuing uncertainty of it all, which was beginning to exasperate some of the more outspoken commentators in the media. A mounting sense of frustration gave rise to newspaper articles, which urged our Generals to "get on with it". Some papers went even further and taunted Hitler about his apparent reluctance to engage in actual warfare.

According to Winston Churchill, in Volume 1 of his book '*The Second World War*', the Regular Army in Britain at that time was 20,000 below strength, including 5,000 officers. The same volume also states that there were known to be 20,000 organised German Nazis in England at this time. Whilst the British were presumably struggling to make good their alarming deficiencies in men and equipment, the Germans were already in the final stages of their preparation for the devastating attacks which they were poised to launch in only a few weeks' time. A foretaste of what was to come was being very effectively demonstrated by their successful invasion of Norway. This took place while we were still at Ludlow.

We had little knowledge about what was happening in the higher echelons of our own army but were increasingly apprehensive about what was happening all around us. Our apparently unscheduled arrival at our Holding Unit had not done much to bolster morale; and the lack of a good deal of very important equipment was equally inauspicious. At one stage, just as we began to wonder whether anyone knew we were there at all, we received the first of two visits, both of which were as unexpected as everything else that came our way.

One morning a Major turned up, accompanied by two Sergeants, to instruct us in the art of hand to hand fighting. I hadn't previously considered this form of combat but its importance was about to be made very clear. Dummies were quickly made up from sacks filled with straw. These were then hung up or laid on the ground, and we gave orders for our men to fix bayonets and charge. "No, no not like that," roared the Major, "like this!" His two burly Sergeants were then given their orders to show us how it should be done. Clearly well practised in such demonstrations they immediately rushed at the targets, filling the air with loud blood-curdling shouts, and ended by plunging their bayonets deep into the 'bodies', not forgetting to twist them thoroughly – an action which they were careful to stress was of the utmost importance. This must have been the one and only time I ever felt the slightest pang of sympathy for the enemy. I presumed that this demonstration of one of the uglier aspects of war should have given us a warning that we could shortly be involved in actual fighting ourselves.

Within a few days another scarcely veiled warning came when our second visitor suddenly turned up as mysteriously as the first. The officer this time had an air of melancholy about him reminiscent of a Funeral Director at work. We were therefore hardly surprised when he told us that he had come from some Army Record office and was anxious to know whether all the men in our Holding Unit had made their wills and if all next of kin had been listed. I was reasonably sure that soon after our original call-up we had all been urged to make our wills as part of the routine of enlistment, but there was something different about this reminder; for some reason there now seemed to be a sense of urgency.

The young in their twenties rarely give much thought to making a will. When, however, what was originally considered to be a vague need suddenly turned into a pressing requirement it begged the question, why? So in all probability, and maybe for the first time, it led to thoughts about death; a subject that was never mentioned and consequently one that none of us as far as I could tell were likely to dwell on for more than a fleeting moment. Like all young everywhere we would be going on, war or no war, until we became older, so there would be plenty of time to think about wills. All the same this episode had ruffled us a bit and we were left with an uneasy feeling that this visiting officer knew something that we didn't.

We had little time for further speculation because within a few days three of us officers were put on standby for an undisclosed destination overseas, one that was not too difficult to guess. So, with another assurance that I would be fully equipped at this next posting, I joined some 220 other Second Lieutenants on an unescorted crossing of the Channel to Cherbourg.

It is curious how, in the midst of anxiety and turmoil, life can very occasionally stand absolutely still. I can vividly recall to this day just such a moment: whilst standing on the deck of this vessel, totally oblivious of what was going on around me, my thoughts had leapt to, not if, but how and when I should make the return journey.

PART TWO

To France

"What did you do in the Great War, daddy?"
Recruiting placard, 1914–1918 war

O N   A R R I V A L   in France we were transported to the main
supply depot at Rouen. The welcoming sight of a vast
Quartermaster's Store lifted my hopes of at last receiving the long
awaited standard equipment, but there was nothing there for officers. "Don't worry," came yet another assurance, "You'll get everything you need once you arrive at the front!"

The 5th Battalion of The Gloucestershire Regiment had left
England in mid-January, and had undergone a period of training at
Thumeries, in northern France, for another two months in very
cold weather. They formed part of first Territorial Army Brigade to
be selected to take over a sector of the Maginot Line.

The renowned Maginot Line, on which France staked her entire
defence from any assault from the east, had taken years to
construct and with its great length and depth was thought to be
impregnable against any attack by land or air. Its hugely impressive
structure, crammed with all the latest technology of the day, could,
however, only prove effective along its actual length and to the
north it stopped at the Franco-Belgian frontier. Presumably France
thought either that the neutrality of Belgium and Holland would
not be violated, or that even if the Low Countries were ever
invaded there would be time for their armies to mount a very effective defence. It was hardly surprising therefore that this enormous
confidence in both the Maginot Line and the strength and fighting
ability of the army led many French people, including their military
leaders, to believe that the threat now posed by Germany was not
nearly as serious as it turned out to be.

The battalion's move to the Saar near Metz towards the end of
March gave them their first opportunity of contact with the French
Army, and, indeed, later with the German forces who attacked
their sector on two occasions.

A Platoon of 'D' Company

On arrival at the front it soon became clear why eight Second
Lieutenants had been sent out to every Regiment serving in
France. Some months earlier the army had created a new rank,
that of Platoon Sergeant-Major (PSM), which was to replace that of

Junior Officers in the command of a platoon – some 26 to 30 men. It had been found in practice that although these PSMs had considerable experience in field craft as well as being competent leaders, most of the men preferred to be led by young officers who held the King's commission however inexperienced they might be; and some of them, as I had already discovered, had barely reached the age of nineteen. Accordingly I soon found myself in charge of a platoon of D Company, all of whom were peacetime volunteers who had had very limited serious training.

On most sectors of the front there had been very little actual fighting. Rather like conditions in the First World War, we had to man defensive positions including trenches, whilst in front of us lay a stretch of no-man's land and somewhere beyond that was the enemy defensive line. Our main activity was concerned with reconnaissance. Our orders were to send out patrols by night to probe the enemy defences, to kill or capture any Germans we might come across, and a last word from our Company Commander – "For heaven's sake, don't get lost!"

These night patrols could be hair-raising experiences. An officer, a sergeant and three or four men would set out from the security of our own lines as silently as possible in the dark with an agreed plan of when and where we would return. The plan had to be adhered to strictly if we were to have any chance of staying alive. The previous week one of our patrols had been ambushed, with disastrous results, so we needed little further incentive to be especially vigilant.

We would thread our way through the partly wooded countryside to probe, not having any clear idea what to expect. We were just as likely to spot an enemy patrol, who were probably hoping as much as we were that we wouldn't suddenly stumble into each other. Every so often we would stop, keep absolutely silent and just listen, straining to hear anything that moved. A mouse rustling in the undergrowth was enough to send the adrenaline racing and the heart thumping. Suddenly, a flare would shoot up into the sky illuminating trees and men, and creating shadows, followed by a burst of rapid fire and then silence and darkness again, as though nothing had happened. Where were we? Could we have gone round in a circle? Had we been out longer than had been arranged? Was I sure of the password, which was changed every night? What on earth were we doing there anyway, other than gaining some sort of experience that we were unlikely ever to use again, and in fact never did? I had even had to borrow a pistol, a weapon I had never fired, to go on these patrols at all. It was indeed a strange feeling to be so inexperienced in this type of warfare and yet be responsible for the lives of at least four others.

Having achieved nothing more than noting what well may have been an enemy defensive position, it was time to return to our own lines. This proved to be even more hazardous than setting out as several of our own men were fairly trigger happy, and tended to rather overdo the challenging routine. What a relief to be back, and what greater relief to learn some ten days later that we were to be replaced on that sector of the front by another regiment.

It was almost inconceivable to me that having reached the front in this war, I should still be unarmed; and I wondered how many others might have been in the same situation. As I came to learn later, I wasn't the only unarmed officer. The Colonel shrugged off my request for at least a pistol of my own with some impatience. I thought at one stage he was going to remind me that there was a war on and that I must expect shortages. His answer was that I should take the rifle from the first soldier in my platoon to be killed and use that, rather than a pistol. This seemed to be the most practical answer and as there was no alternative way to get armed, I had to accept it, including the dismal way in which it might come about. As it happened, I should have been much more at ease with a rifle anyway, being well acquainted with the weapon, one with which I had had a particular success shooting at Bisley in a competition less than a year before.

Intensive Training at Auby

The battalion left Metz and the Saar on 23rd April, returning to the previous training area near Auby – some three miles north of Douai. In this flat and rather uninspiring part of France we came across a number of French civilians who, though friendly, seemed to go about their business with hardly a care in the world. This display of apparent unconcern about the war was in sharp contrast to the very serious attitude now taken by our Colonel concerning our fitness for battle. Our time at the front had been an eye-opener, and it had become only too clear that many of our Territorial Battalion were under-trained as well as unfit. The Colonel ordered intensive training to start immediately with special emphasis on both physical fitness and firing practice. On the firing range few of my platoon seemed capable of hitting the target. I asked one man, whose firing was exceptionally wild, what he thought he was aiming at. He replied, "I've never been allowed to fire a rifle before, Sir, because of my squint."

Amidst all this hectic training we all managed to find some time to write letters home. One of the least attractive duties officers were obliged to perform was that of censoring the letters of the men. I always felt ill at ease having to read such personal letters to wives, girl-friends and relatives, and found it difficult to shrug off a guilty feeling of looking through a keyhole; but what I suppose we should now call invasion of privacy was sadly necessary. There would always be ome unthinking idiot who would actually write the name of the place where we were or had just come from; not that I thought the enemy would have gained much from seeing such letters as they probably knew exactly where we were anyway. Many of the letters were highly sentimental and often bore the word SWALK on the back of the envelope. This, I learnt, stood for 'Sealed With A Loving Kiss', a message that was far too tame for others, who preferred the more robust approach embodied in the word NORWICH – meaning '(K)Nickers Off Ready When I Come Home'. Reflecting on this one day, I wondered how a Bishop of Norwich might sign his letters.

May 1940 – a significant month

The twelve days we had spent in intensive training certainly resulted in some improvement in our overall efficiency, but we were still very amateur and a long way off becoming anything like a professional unit. Time, however, was not on our side and there was no opportunity for further training because the Phoney War suddenly came to an abrupt end.

The tenth of May, 1940 was indeed a memorable day. It was the day on which Germany launched a full-scale offensive against the Allies. On the same day in Britain Winston Churchill became Prime Minister and immediately set about forming a War Cabinet; and on this day in France the French Government was in disarray, with 10% to 15% of the French army on leave.

By this time Norway and most of Sweden had been lost to the enemy. The valuable experience gained from their Scandinavian campaign was about to lead the Germans to even greater success in France as they adopted the same strategy of attacking at speed with armoured divisions. In one of the hottest months of May for some years, they quickly broke through into neutral Holland and Belgium. In response to urgent appeals from the Belgians, most of the British Expeditionary Force, under the command of general

Gort but subject to the French Supreme Command, were ordered to hasten northwards.

BELGIUM

On 13th May, our Battalion embussed in troop-carrying transport and moved north into Belgium, following leading Divisions of the British Expeditionary Force (BEF). In spite of being machine gunned from the air *en route*, we managed to reach our destination early that morning in the Forest of Soignies, a few miles south of Brussels. During the time it took to arrive there, news kept coming in about the continuing German thrust into Belgium, so it was hardly surprising that almost as soon as we reached our destination further orders were received for us to withdraw. The word 'Retreat' was never heard. The British army, I was assured, never retreats. From time to time, however, the army may engage in 'Tactical or Strategic Withdrawals'. This euphemistic expression, presumably intended to minimise any loss of morale among the troops, wore thinner as it was repeated each day.

So preoccupied was I with the turmoil of these withdrawals, mostly at night, that it never occurred to me at the time that we were passing through the very area south of Brussels in which my ancestor, General or Colonel as he was then, Sir Philip had commanded the Gloucestershire Regiment in the battle of Waterloo in 1815. The contrast between then and 1940 couldn't have been more marked. At Quatres Bras the Glosters, the regiment of the 28th of Foot, had formed square and held their ground against repeated attacks by Napoleon's infantry and cavalry. Now we were in the act of withdrawing from an enemy we had hardly seen and with whom we were yet to engage in actual combat.

Three days after reaching our first position near Brussels, our Battalion had already withdrawn to a position well to the south and had marched thirty miles in twenty-four hours without sleep and with only one small meal. Our fourth day in Belgium, after another long march, brought us still further south to a canal at Lessines, which we had to cross and behind which we were to man a defensive position on the following day. More digging-in; more establishing of communications; more regrouping and certainly more frustration as this sequence of withdrawals effectively eliminated any opportunity for sleep.

Why, we wondered, couldn't we hold some position or other and stand firm and fight? I couldn't be sure of the answer at the time although it became increasingly obvious. Enemy planes, bomber and spotter planes, were everywhere while there seemed to be very few of ours around. The Luftwaffe appeared to be in complete control. On the ground the BEF was without a single armoured division, having only one Army Tank Brigade consisting of 17 light tanks and 100 'infantry tanks', most of the latter being equipped with nothing more than machine guns. These light tanks may have been good for reconnaissance work but were no match for the heavily armed powerful German tanks, which seemed capable of sweeping away anything in their paths. The Boyes anti-tank rifles with their .505 bullets could, and indeed did, score direct hits on enemy tanks, yet the latter never faltered in their advance.

Having spent three successive nights in withdrawals, we at last had orders to hold yet another defensive line 'to the last man and the last round'. It must have been some seven years before and probably in some training session with my Officers Training Corps at school that I first heard this chilling command. As boys, and far removed from any reality of war, we found a strange unreality in conjuring up a picture of one brave fellow, his dead companions all around him, about to fire his final round before, presumably, being killed himself. Now it was real. The command could hardly be more dramatic; fighting talk indeed, but as we had already been given it twice before and on each occasion had been ordered to withdraw before we had fired a single shot, it was beginning to lose whatever force it ever had.

Now, along a stretch of the canal at Lessines, we actually held our designated section for a night and most of a day. For the first time we could clearly see enemy troops marching through a clearing in the wood opposite; being given the order to halt, and then to split up into small groups, probably to find the most convenient place to cross over. We were thus able to engage them in small arms fire and to lob grenades over the canal at them long before they were able to cross.

I recall admiring the way in which one of my platoon was adept at throwing these grenades, and learnt later that he was a keen village cricketer who certainly knew how to return balls from boundary. I even borrowed a rifle myself for a brief spell for some real live target practice, which was just as well because several of the enemy had somehow managed to cross the river and were in easy range. The main body of their troops, however, withdrew into the wood on the other side, where we lost sight of them, but from where they began to launch heavy mortar fire at our positions.

In this first actual engagement with the enemy one of my platoon was killed. I managed to grab his rifle only to find that the bullet that had killed him must have glanced off the barrel rendering it useless. I doubt whether our battalion was particularly effective in holding up any part of the German advance in that sector because our stand there was short-lived, and once again we had orders to withdraw. This order was becoming increasingly depressing and even more so now because we found our progress hampered by hundreds of refugees, who trailed alongside us carrying everything they could and with very little idea about where they might end up. Old men, women and children began to clutter up the roads in a desperate effort to put themselves as far away from the advancing enemy as possible, yet with little real hope of achieving more than postponing the day when they would eventually be overtaken. I never found out what happened to them, but those that survived the horrors of their journey, which included being machine-gunned occasionally from the air, must have wondered whether their efforts were really worth the cost of the dreadful suffering they had to endure.

It is difficult to describe the total disarray caused by the massive withdrawal of the British and French armies compounded by the streams of civilian refugees that grew larger each day. The Germans had little difficulty in extracting the maximum advantage from the chaos, which they themselves had initiated; especially as their spotter planes were able to pinpoint the position of any large concentrations of vehicles or troops. On one such occasion some two hundred British troop carriers were spotted converging on a bridge and all were blown to bits by bombers.

Long before the war began the Germans were making use of 'Fifth Columnists', a term that arose during the Spanish Civil War. (It is related that, in 1936, when General Mola was besieging Madrid he was asked whether he thought his four columns were sufficient to take the city. He replied that he was relying on a fifth column of sympathisers within. The term has consequently come to mean traitors, infiltrators and spies.) Fifth Columnists were used widely by the Germans in all the countries they invaded, and, indeed in Britain. Reports reached us in Belgium of a German soldier being caught dressed in the habit of a nun; and of another one wearing British uniform with an official looking armband who was belatedly caught at a cross-roads directing British army convoys along a road which would have certainly lead them into an ambush. There were also a significant number of civilian Nazi sympathisers in strategic positions spread all over the battle areas as well as behind our lines. There was no knowing who these innocent looking people were, but the damage they did by transmitting information to the enemy must have been enormous. Confronted by this additional problem, and hampered by out-of-date maps, it was a wonder that we managed to make the progress that we did - especially as most vehicle movements took place after dark and without lights.

DUNKIRK

By the 27th May, we had almost reached the outskirts of Dunkirk. It was the day on which the Commander-in-Chief – General Gort – received orders to evacuate as many of the B.E.F as possible. Some 8000 had already crossed the Channel to England, and the successful evacuation of so many more thousands was going to depend on the success or failure of the two German pincer movements, which then threatened the retreating army. The war in France was virtually over, and all that remained was to ensure that as many men as possible should make the treacherous crossing home.

As we approached Dunkirk it became clear that we were not destined to take part in any evacuation – as yet anyway. The town was already densely overcrowded with troops and equipment and the Brigadier in charge decided that the danger from bombers on such concentrations was too great. We were therefore ordered to proceed southwards to make every effort to stem, or at least delay, the German advance.

With morale at its lowest level, hungry and utterly exhausted from so many consecutive nights without any sleep, we probably couldn't have repulsed an attack by a sheep. However, orders are orders and so south we went for some twelve miles, skirting round the small town of Wormhout to another little town further south called Arneke. That night our Battalion was attacked by tanks, heavy mortar fire and infantry rushes. How we managed to hold our positions here I just cannot remember, but I do recall that in this engagement we managed to inflict some damage on the enemy, though at the cost of quite a number of casualties ourselves. When all seemed lost we were ordered to go to the support of other companies in the defence of the small village of Ledringham, only a short distance away and just over a mile from Wormhout.

Massacre at Wormhout

Here I must record an event of which I was, thankfully, totally ignorant at the time, and which I only came to learn about in any real detail from reading a book almost exactly sixty-one years later called 'Massacre on the Road to Dunkirk: Wormhout 1940' by Leslie Aitken. This book relates the story of what was probably the first atrocity of the war involving British troops, and describes what survivors who were eyewitnesses at the time were not able to relate until a few years later. The book itself was not published until 1977.

The regiment involved was the Royal Warwickshire, who were on our left flank, and who were overrun by the Waffen SS or Adolf

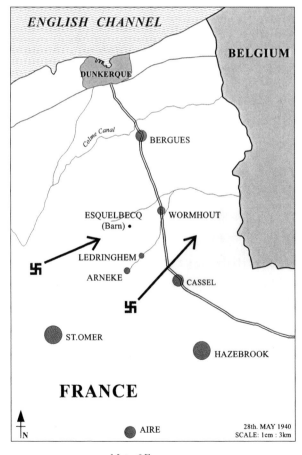

Map of France, 1940.

Hitler Regiment. In this engagement on 28th May, about one hundred prisoners were taken, some having their identity discs removed. These men were herded into a small barn just southwest of Wormhout. An officer with them complained to the Germans that the barn was far too small to accommodate that number of men. He was brusquely told that there was nothing to worry about as "There'll be plenty of room where they are going!" - an answer which the officer took to indicate an eventual prisoner-of-war camp. Their captors meanwhile appeared to be busy conferring with each other. Suddenly, amidst much shouting, five men were ordered to come out of the barn and go to a point about twenty yards away. Here the five men were ordered to stand in a row facing five German soldiers. They were then told to face about, whereupon each was shot in the back of the head. The bodies were left where they had fallen, and there was further shouting for another five men to come out.

By this time those in the barn had heard shots and a few of them had actually seen through cracks in the walls what had happened to their comrades. The horror of this cold-blooded killing and the sudden realisation that that was to be the fate of them all was leading to pandemonium, but not before another five men had emerged, been directed to a place a little distance from the others and lined up before another firing squad. These five, however, on being ordered to face about all swivelled round to face their executioners at the very moment they too were shot in the head. Further shouting for another five to come out coincided with a torrential downpour of rain, and brought about such a scene of terrifying alarm in the barn that no more would venture forth. After another brief conference, the Germans, to avoid getting soaked and anxious not to delay their advance any longer, stormed the barn using automatic weapons to kill those standing at the entrance and to spray bullets at random into the remainder inside. Satisfied that all were dead, they left.

Unbelievably, a few survived this massacre. They did so either by somehow managing to escape, or by feigning death under the bodies of their friends who had been killed in the initial onslaught. Out of the original hundred, fifteen survived – a few of them long enough for their story to be told; to be authenticated; and finally to be written up by their padre.

Sadly, massacres hardly rate very highly as news any longer. We were to learn of many more, which took place during, and, indeed, after the war, some of which were perpetrated by countries other than Germany. This one, however, was made all the more unforgivable by the fact that the Germans had been showering leaflets on our troops urging them to give themselves up in a struggle that was "hopeless", adding that any thoughts they may have had about Germans shooting prisoners were totally false as they treated prisoners with respect. The leaflet ended with the words: "We are not savages!"

Going to war at all presupposes an acceptance, or at least an understanding, that wounds or death itself may come in battle. To meet death in cold blood must be one of the worst ways to die and one which, if they ever came to know it, would cause the deepest distress to relatives. This may be one of the reasons why the publication of this book did not take place until nearly forty years after the event.

Impending attack

The massacre itself was actually taking place just over a mile away from where our D Company of the 5th Gloucestershire Regiment, or rather what was left of it, were taking up their position on the same day – 28th May. It was in fact happening between us and our possible escape route to Dunkirk. At the time we were close enough to Wormhout to see the town being heavily bombed; to hear the high-pitched screams of the falling bombs and to hear the shattering noise of the ensuing explosions. Later that evening it became strangely quiet, and I began to wonder if there was going to be any opportunity to catch up on desperately needed sleep. But, no, hardly had I returned from checking the position of my depleted platoon when I heard the loud rumbling noise of a tank. Crouching down, I was close enough to see the white cross on its side and even to hear its crew talking to each other. I still cannot understand how, even in the gathering dusk, all of them failed to see me. The sudden appearance of this tank was an obvious pointer to an impending attack, yet everything went curiously quiet once more.

Taking stock of the situation that evening was a major problem. How immensely helpful it would have been to have had the use of a map, compass and binoculars - I didn't even have a pistol. The last order received - to hold a section of the line around Ledringham – was coupled with a warning that an attack was likely from the east. As well as the Royal Warwickshire Regiment, the 4th (TA) Battalion

Oxfordshire and Buckinghamshire Regiment nearby, and to the south was the 2nd Battalion of the Gloucestershire Regiment (Regulars) was succeeding in putting up a magnificent defence of the town of Cassel. This action subsequently earned them the praise even of the enemy, and it must have made a major contribution to the delaying of the German advance on Dunkirk. This enemy attack, however, was not from the east but from the southwest, and was intended to cut off any hopes that any of us might have entertained of reaching Dunkirk ourselves.

The vital order for us to withdraw and make our way to Dunkirk had already been given but, as was learnt years later, it arrived twenty-four hours late because the messenger had been held up by enemy action. Maybe the order couldn't have been sent by radio because so much equipment had already been destroyed, or maybe the enemy had succeeded in breaking our codes, but by the time it did arrive all of us had been completely surrounded. About a third of the already depleted Battalion who did receive the order in time somehow reached Dunkirk, making their way through territory mainly held by the enemy. Another third of the original Battalion were either killed or severely wounded; the remainder were floundering about in the area where I was without much hope of achieving anything.

By the side of the road and with few men from one depleted Section of my platoon, not sure where the rest of our D Company was because there had been no communication for some hours, I was beginning to feel somewhat isolated. It was an eerie feeling that lasted all night, made all the more eerie by a strange quietness. Having still had no chance of sleep, I tried to pull myself together to face yet another dawn. There was some machine gun fire but it seemed a long way off. As it became lighter there was some movement, or so I thought, in a small wooden hut next to the ditch by the road, and something prompted me to go and investigate. It was empty, but as I was leaving it there was a resounding explosion. The next thing I remembered, presumably some minutes later, was lying on my back in the ditch and opening my eyes to see a German officer pointing his pistol straight down at me and shouting at me to get out. The hut had completely disintegrated and there was no sign of the men who had been near me. There was blood on my battle-dress and some on me, but I seemed to have escaped anything more serious than some cuts and a large splinter in my arm. I crawled out and was immediately searched for weapons.

They were slow to believe that I hadn't any and gave me a second thorough going over.

So ended for me an inglorious, yet brief, experience of fighting a war, and so began early on the morning of 29th May 1940, an indefinite period of captivity.

Post office telegrams – 'believed missing' and 'is a prisoner of war'.

PART THREE

Caught! Life in German Camps

"Shoulder to aching shoulder, side by side,
They trudged away from life's broad wealds of light"

Siegfried Sassoon

Map of prisoner-of-war camps mentioned in the book

As with most of the others caught at the same time, the thought of becoming a prisoner-of-war had never occurred to me. Consequently I was dazed as well as utterly exhausted. Fortunately, the rounding-up process must have taken some time – I never learnt how long – I had fallen asleep on the ground. I awoke to see a gathering of officers and men, a few of whom I recognised. They all seemed to have that glazed, listless look that was characteristic of the newly captured. A German Officer came up to me and said in perfect English: "For you the war is over, are you glad?" About ten of us were then ordered to line up against a wall for no obvious reason. It was just as well that at the time I hadn't learnt off a similar order given, soon after they were captured, to fifteen men of the Cheshire Regiment, who were then all shot. The purpose of the exercise for us, however, was only for a further search in case any of us had managed to secrete anything that could possibly be used as a weapon. I tried to find out what had happened to the reminder of my platoon but no one there knew. It was some time before I learnt that nearly all of them had been taken prisoner. Meanwhile the separation from one's men, and the inability to do anything about it, was the first sharp indication of the invidious nature of captivity.

'The Great Trek'

That afternoon we were herded into groups and ordered to march behind a number of similar groups of French. So began 'The Great Trek', which was to last thirteen days, during which we covered over two hundred miles. In the early stages there was little or no food, though as we progressed supplies increased. I cannot recall our route but it took us through a part of France and Belgium, and so into Germany where we stopped for a brief spell near Coblenz.

Each day, dispirited and often hungry, we set off on this dreary journey wearing the same battle-dress, shirt, underwear, socks and boots, with no possessions other than those we had on us at the time of our capture. Each day we marched or rather walked, or trudged at three hourly stretches for between fourteen and eighteen miles. Feet became sore; and the early lack of food made us weak, yet on we went. If anyone fell by the wayside, quite incapable of continuing, he was left where he fell. On one occasion such a casualty was bayoneted where he lay. One other time, after we had moved on a bit, a guard was despatched to where one of our number had collapsed. We heard a shot, and the guard caught up with us later. The stronger amongst us tried to do what we could to help those who were finding the going particularly hard, for by then the penalty for not keeping up couldn't have been made clearer.

Our numbers seemed to vary from day to day; sometimes there were about three hundred of us and at other times nearer two thousand. Each night we slept in the same clothes; in barns, churches, schools, but mostly in open fields and occasionally in drenching rain without any cover. These night camps sometimes provided an opportunity to scrounge around for the most urgent necessity – some sort of receptacle for drinks, soup or any food that might come our way. An old discarded tin, even rusty became a prized possession. More food did eventually become available, mostly soup and bread. These were sometimes supplemented by offerings which were pressed on us by civilians in villages through which we passed, who probably had very little food themselves. Whenever any food was distributed by the Germans preference was always given to the French, so we were not sorry to see the last of our allies, when they left us for some other destination after the first week or so. In one school where we spent a night it was possible to get a shower and even to wash a few clothes, hoping they would be dry for wearing again the following morning. A few of us actually managed to shave.

The latter half of this trek was less traumatic than the first; we were now well clear of the battle zones and so no longer were to encounter men lying face down where they had died with their tin hats still on their heads, nor bloated cattle with their stiffened legs pointing to the sky, and it was a relief to be far away from the stench of rotting flesh. The foot-slogging over such a distance had been a gruelling experience and now, thankfully, it was coming to an end. Such journeys, combining one's own physical discomfort with a close view of the trials of others, tend to haunt the memory.

On entering Germany everyone was subject to yet another thorough search; all knives, tin hats and what remained of anything which could possibly be classified as warlike was taken away. Thus we arrived at Coblenz for a train journey along the Mosel valley to

Trier. By a curious irony of fate this was the very same journey, although in the opposite direction, which had been provisionally arranged for me to take in September 1939 as a result of winning a Wine Trade Essay Competition that year. I had been assured that the award, with all expenses paid, would be kept for me until after the war. As it was, I found myself being herded with about a hundred others into a cattle truck designed to take '40 Hommes et 8 Chevaux'. Securely locked in and with no window through which to see the beautiful valley with its vine-covered slopes full of endless rows of newly formed grapes, I began to wonder if I would ever make the same journey in happier circumstances, or indeed ever want to repeat it.

On arrival at Trier we were transferred to a train with some very old-fashioned carriages which were to take us to our final destination. The whole journey was a nightmare but worse was to come. At one of our frequent unscheduled stops in the middle of nowhere, two officers made a dash for it in the gathering darkness. Unluckily for them the guards were very alert and the two, who had almost reached the end of a field, suddenly found themselves in the glare of a powerful searchlight from the train. The guards shouted, the two put their hands up and there was an immediate burst of fire. The swathe of bullets must have virtually sliced one of them in half, as he jack-knifed forward, his head falling to his knees. I had seen some gruesome sights during the last few weeks but there was something especially horrifying in witnessing a cold-blooded killing, even in wartime. It was also a grim warning of how they would deal with escaping prisoners-of-war.

Laufen Camp

It was a great relief when this train journey ended, and when shortly afterwards we reached our first camp at Laufen in Bavaria. The building had originally been the old Bishop's Palace but it had more recently been used for Polish prisoners. With its five storeys it was an impressive structure, at least from the outside. It was here, however, that we first began to feel a much stronger sense of captivity. Up until then we had been largely in the open; now we were surrounded by two eight-feet high barbed wire fences running parallel to each other and separated by seven feet, the gaps being filled with coils and coils of more barbed wire. A trip wire, a further six feet inside this perimeter marked the boundary, and anyone crossing it risked being shot at. Sentry boxes about twenty-five feet

Prisoner ID card.

high were spaced at regular intervals and were manned day and night, being equipped with machine guns and searchlights which would sweep their beams to the boundary and round the camp throughout the night.

A bleak Christmas at Laufen Camp.

Living

Officers had long since been separated from other ranks, and at Laufen there were nearly two thousand of us. The converted barracks were designed to accommodated far fewer. We subalterns were located on the second floor in a fairly large room with thirty-three three-tier beds, ninety-nine of us to the room, whose only heating was from a single standing stove. The palliasses on which we slept were half-filled with straw. We each had a locker, and there were a few wooden tables with an adequate number of three-legged stools.

Many believed even at that stage, in mid-1940, that some sort of compromise treaty would be signed and that we should all be "home for Christmas". This optimistic hope was by no means new. In its early days, the First World War was not expected to last long and, having started in August 1914, many had thought it would be over by Christmas. Of almost every war since, the same thought has been expressed, with Christmas always the perceived time by which to be home. This was indeed a forlorn hope for us because, as it turned out, we were destined to remain at Laufen for nine long months.

For several of these months we wore the same clothes, and still lacked most of the basic necessities such as toothbrushes, nail scissors, razors or combs; not that we needed the latter for long

53

because after two or three weeks the order came through for us all to have our heads shaved – in case of lice. A friend who had been a sheep farmer assured us that there was nothing to worry about as within three months we should all have a much better head of hair than before; that as it was summer we wouldn't get cold, and that we were lucky not to have been ordered into a cleansing dip as well! Before any shearing began, we had all been issued with new identity discs; had all been questioned and had our essential details recorded and had been photographed. Afterwards we were photographed without hair.

Eating

One of the few words of German I was to learn, though not from choice as the coarse guttural sounds of the language lack all charm for me, was 'ersatz' meaning substitute. A great number of things in Germany were indeed ersatz, and the first example of this was the so-called coffee that was dished up each morning. This concoction was made from acorns, and apart from being brown and occasion-ally warm bore no other resemblance to real coffee. At midday we were given soup, a thin watery liquid in which a few very old pota-toes had apparently met their end by drowning. Once a week we had meat in the soup as well as the long-past-it potatoes. We were never sure what this meat actually was but one thing was certain – there would be very little of it. On one memorable occasion, a final stir of this grisly gruel containing gristle and other unmentionable parts – nothing was wasted – caused a jawbone to surface, complete with a row of teeth. One of our number had once been a horse dealer and upon closer examination he was able to establish and announce the age of the animal. We all rather wished he hadn't.

In the evening there would be more 'coffee'. We were also each issued with a 400-gram loaf of brown bread, but this had to last for five days. It was mostly eaten dry, as there was nothing to spread on it.

We rapidly became much weaker, both physically, having a noticeable lack of energy, and also mentally; as I began to learn, the brain needs sustenance as well as the rest of the body. We began to lose the will to do anything that required any sort of effort. Taking some daily exercise by walking around the compound a few times and then ascending two flights of stairs seemed like climbing a mountain. We hankered after somewhere to sit comfortably, as a three-legged wooden stool with nothing to rest one's back against anything fell far short of any relief. There was only one thing for it – to lie on one's bed. Many hours that summer must have been whiled away in this horizontal attitude until the moment came to stand up again. This brought instant dizziness. It was disturbing to have to stand a minute or so to regain balance and composure; an experience that caused a good deal of consternation.

Personalities

All this time we had kept very much together within our various regiments but as time went on, and through living in such close proximity with each other, we began to get to know a number of our contemporaries in other units and in this way started to form new groups whilst retaining existing bonds within our own regiments.

There were usually two parades each day, morning and evening, for us all to be counted. Sometimes, however, there could be a snap parade even in the middle of the night. The day parades were often followed by periods of exercise during which we would walk round and round an open area always, though I never discovered why, in an anticlockwise direction. Conversation in these early days seemed mainly concerned with how we had come to be caught at all and more especially why. Who was to blame? Where was our artillery? What had happened to our air cover? Pointless rhetorical questions to which there were no answers, nor ever would be; but they expressed frustration, resentment and sometimes anger. Such were the snatches of conversation that drifted across the exercise area as we continued aimlessly round and round. How often I caught the words: " If only…"

There was one young subaltern who had lived in Jersey for many years, but was in England when the war was declared. Because of his local knowledge of the island he was selected to be landed at night on a Jersey beach, whence he was to glean some vital information. In almost total darkness he managed to reach the beach only to realise shortly afterwards that the submarine had landed in Guernsey, which was unfamiliar to him and where he was quickly arrested.

Then there was the only man in camp to have pyjamas. He had been duty officer with his unit in Dover; had gone to bed one night only to receive an urgent summons in the early hours of the following morning. He had rushed to put his uniform on over his pyjamas, and within a few hours had crossed to Calais with his regiment. Almost immediately he was involved in fighting which resulted in him being taken prisoner.

Cut off from the world

During the first few months at Laufen morale remained at a very low level. The only way we could glean news about the conduct of the war was through those who were able to read German newspapers, which were filled with accounts of continuing and outstanding successes of their forces on land, at sea and in the air. Everything seemed to be going their way. It was difficult to believe that German forces had succeeded in sweeping across Holland, Belgium and France in a matter of some three weeks, a victory they had failed to achieve during the four long years of bitter fighting in the First World War in spite of the horrendous loss of life on both sides. It was equally unbelievable that their new success had not been followed up by an immediate invasion of England. Maybe the Germans had surprised themselves with the comparative ease and sheer speed of their advance, and consequently were unprepared to extend their operations further at that time. They were certainly not prepared for the number of prisoners who had fallen into their hands; nor indeed at that time was the British Red Cross. It took several months before any organisation on either side became at all effective.

This interim period was a very difficult one; it was like being stuck in the doldrums at sea. We were becalmed in the midst of a Europe at war, knowing virtually nothing about what was happening all around us, and in our current state solely concerned with ourselves and whatever might contribute to our survival. These uninspiring days and weeks could occasionally be enlivened by the simplest of diversions. We were once asked by some of our own senior officers to provide information about our peacetime occupations together with any qualifications or degrees we may have acquired. This request led to a riot of highly imaginative answers. Sadly, I have forgotten all of these, except for the one from an officer who claimed that he had full-time employment as a "Greaser of Channel Swimmers - now temporarily out of work". The request for information had, however, a serious purpose - to seek out those with sufficient knowledge about any subject, together with the ability, and willingness, to talk about it, in an effort to initiate some sort of interest in an atmosphere of unrelieved military monotony.

The 'University'

There were neither books nor writing paper, nor indeed any of the essentials of normal civilised life, so we were obliged to resort to our own initiative in improvisation by making use of what talent there was available – and there was plenty. We were all reasonably well educated and had all been involved for however short a period in some profession or industry, or had pursued some hobby about which we could be persuaded to talk. Whoever was responsible for initiating this enquiry deserved the gratitude of us all because it quickly led to the establishment of what later came to be known as a "University." Even more importantly, it offered an end to the frustration of having little to do.

A sufficient number of officers were willing to hold forth on their pet subjects, so the 'University' was founded with all speed. In spite of a lack of almost all the materials required, including paper, an initial programme was devised for the first week. The talks would take place mostly in the various rooms, or dormitories, where each of us spent much of the day anyway. The project was widely supported and the success of the first week led to a much fuller programme of talks or lectures designed to be spread over the next two or three months.

As the weeks passed by, more volunteer lecturers emerged and the range of talks increased considerably. They included art, music, literature, languages, accountancy, law, estate management, theology, geology, philosophy, astronomy, psychology and many more, to which were added a number of hobbies. One of these I found of particular interest; it was all about bees. I became so enthusiastic that in one of the two letters we were allowed to write each month, I asked my rather surprised parents if they could possibly send me a book about bee-keeping. When, some two years later, a large volume arrived for me, I had long forgotten all about bees and wondered what on earth had prompted my parents to send such a book. Luckily there were others who had a more lasting interest in the subject.

I had volunteered myself to help in any talk on wine. As soon as the subject was listed on one of the weekly programmes, it became oversubscribed to such an extent that one of the two larger 'public' rooms had to be set aside for the talk. These rooms were used either for church services or, later on, for concerts. The thought of a large audience in such a room filled me with foreboding, especially as I had had such a comparatively short experience in the subject. Fortunately three others quickly came to the fore, each of whom had much more background knowledge about wine than I had time to acquire. It was decided that we deliver the lecture by each speaking briefly on some aspects of wine, and then as a panel invite questions. Our talk seemed to be well received but I could hardly believe the first question, which came from the back of the room and which vividly recalled my last talk on wine, in the Chapel of Horfield Prison in 1938: "Can the panel tell us how to make hooch?"

On the whole morale took an upward turn because it had now become possible to fill in at least part of the day by attending some talk or other. In fact it amounted to much more than just filling in time as many of the talks were extremely good, and it would have been foolish not to have grasped the opportunity to learn something from those who were able to speak with such obvious authority on so wide a range of subjects.

One very significant talk was given by one of our doctors, who told us that the calorific value of the amount of food we were getting was just sufficient to sustain life. If we were to continue much longer without any increase we would surely be heading for a variety of medical problems. The least of these, he explained, would probably be shrinkage in the size of our stomachs; one way in which nature compensated for the conditions we were in. Only one or two rather portly majors welcomed this news. The only cheering thing he had to say for us younger ones was that we had a very much better chance of surviving the current regime than those who were in their forties. There were a number around this age, for whom I had much sympathy; some were clearly finding the going rather hard, especially one who had spent four years of the First World War in German prison camps. This Major gave a very interesting talk on his experiences, but we found it almost incredible that anyone should have spent that length of time as a prisoner. Little did we know. This talk and the more practical one from the doctor led us into a new phase of even deeper gloom. Not for long, however, because it was just about then that the first letters arrived from Britain.

Letters from home

These early letters mostly expressed relief from parents, wives and relatives that we were alive, and touched on the long period of acute anxiety they had gone through without any news other than that reported to them by the War Office: that we were "missing". Letters from home were enormously important to us. It is really only to family that one can communicate freely, because it is only family that can be trusted completely and who can be relied upon to understand in a way that is beyond the capacity of even the closest of friends. Having friends around was the one saving grace that enabled each of us to survive through all the tribulations of the life we were destined to lead for several years. But, even with the best of them, there would always be a number of matters that couldn't, and maybe shouldn't be discussed. Now, the only communication with family was by writing letters restricted in length and subject to censorship. Yet it was possible and at times enjoyable to be able to use some of those expressions that so often unaccountably develop within families, and which would probably have little if any meaning to anyone else. Sometimes the German censor would suspect some sort of code; and in a way that's what it was.

Most of the letters we received were full of encouragement, and made very little reference to the increasing hardship developing in Britain as the war dragged on. All incoming letters had been through the censor's hands at home; consequently there was no real news even about friends. One of us received a letter with the information that "*James has joined the *******, and is probably on his way to ******. Rupert is now in the Navy and is serving on HMS ********and I think is shortly off to ********.*"

If any of us developed a conscience about our own letters home being too concerned with ourselves and our own needs, it would have been allayed to some extent by a few of the letters we received, such as this one on the writing paper of a well-known London Club: "*I'm so sorry to hear of your misfortune, it may be a blessing in disguise. Life here is fast becoming intolerable. Everything is grossly expensive, especially cigars, whilst vintage port has completely vanished. It took me two hours yesterday to buy a few razor blades and some caviar. Never see anyone I know, and the place is full of infernal foreigners.*"

Another letter from a Lieutenant Colonel informed his 23 year old son that he was a disgrace to the family to have been taken prisoner; that he was now cut off from all his inheritance, and should henceforth no longer consider himself to be his son. Before the end of the war it was learnt that this same Lt.Col., who was later promoted to Brigadier, was himself taken prisoner by the Japanese at the fall of Singapore.

Less serious but still disturbing was a letter from one officer's Aunt Julia. "*I envy you all the time you now have for study. I hear you have a university, what a chance for you to get a degree. Only the other day I met a man who'd been a prisoner in the last war – of course, he's slightly queer in the head – but now speaks seven languages…PS John's birthday party at the Savoy last week…Saw your fiancée there…such an attractive girl and she was having a tremendous success with some of our brave fighter boys, I wish you could have seen her…*"

A real classic, however, came from one subaltern's great-aunt, an American, who wrote: "*I wonder if you have met Herr Himmler yet? Such charming man. I dined with him before the war…I'm sure if he knew where you were, he would see you were properly looked after.*" (Himmler, in 1940, was head of the Gestapo, the German secret police, and was hanged as a war criminal after the Nuremberg War Crimes Trials that followed the war.)

One day I found myself amongst a few others who had each received a letter out of the blue from Holland. Somehow our names must have been noted by a Dutch organisation, which encouraged their members to write to British prisoners-of-war. My correspondent was a cheerful girl, who wrote a delightful letter without any reference to the appalling conditions in Holland. She later sent me an attractive photograph of herself and asked if there was anything I should like her to send me. I thanked her for her kind thought but declined as rumours had already reached us – later proved to be true – that the food situation in Holland was such that many people there had resorted to eating tulip bulbs.

Hunger

Whilst some experience of real hunger had caught up with us too, it was probably less severe that that suffered by those in the counties occupied by Germany at that time. It was certainly as nothing to the hunger that prevailed in various other parts of the world, especially in Africa. In this new millennium, hardly a month goes by without some heart-rending scene being transmitted on to our television screens from a drought-stricken or war-torn country showing us in vivid detail what the effects of starvation are, especially upon children and the elderly. In 1940 in Germany, we were yet to see these appalling scenes, but we were to learn first hand at least something about what it feels like and what it means to be truly hungry.

To most of us this was a very new experience and as it was one

which recurred from time to time when it did, it tended to preoc-
cupy our minds to the exclusion of anything else. We might have
come to realise very much sooner that our situation was far from
unique in the world, if only we had had at the time recourse to
books and had been able to read about some historical sieges and
their effects. One in particular would have been very appropriate.
In his autobiography, - 'Among Others' – Lord Elton wrote about
the siege of Kut:

> Gradually hunger, and especially the lack of anything sweet, grew
> to colour the imagination, waking and sleeping. These ravenous
> yearnings obtruded themselves on everything one thought or did.
> One would lay a sentimental novel down, as hero was gathering
> heroine into his arms, to speculate on what the lovesick pair were
> likely to eat for lunch – as to which, alas! the novel would be
> silent. One would compose imaginary menus, and gloatingly,
> course by course, talk over the heroic meals of the past. One
> thought by day and dreamed by night, not of the victory of the
> relieving force, but of mutton cutlets, of York ham, above all, of
> being let loose in a confectioners…Leathery Majors of the Indian
> Army would look up dreamily from a hand of bridge in the
> Mess…and these hard-bitten warriors were not thinking of
> corkscrews and bottles of whisky. They were planning to sit down
> with a tablespoon to a pot of jam

By the late autumn of 1940, the British Red Cross had become
much better organised and with hundreds of volunteer workers in
Britain they were fully geared to cope with the needs of British prisoners-of-war. I recall the work of the Red Cross throughout my
years in Germany with the greatest admiration. The way in which
they maintained a supply of food parcels over so long a period was
truly remarkable. This continuous boost to the meagre and dreary
diet on which we were existing was vital to our physical health and
did a great deal for morale. Whilst appreciating their tireless efforts
we also felt frustration at not being able to express adequately our
gratitude – anyway at the time – to so many in the UK who were
working so hard to ensure that we received our supplies.

With the help of the Red Cross parcels our overall diet improved
a bit, but it was still well below what we really needed. By using
some of the empty tins we could attempt to cook something, but
this would be on a rare occasion when none of the other ninety-
eight in the room wanted to do so at the same time and there was

space on the one and only stove. I never thought I would hear an officer from one of our most respected regiments shout out: "There's something boiling over in a boot polish tin!" For some reason the sheer incongruity of this warning shout has remained with me all these years, perhaps because it was so typical of the life we were leading at the time. Equally impossible to have imagined earlier was the sight of another such officer picking up potato peelings from the floor and washing them carefully before eating them raw. How true was J.B. Priestley's comment when he wrote in one of his Self–Selected Essays: "You have to be hungry to appreciate a potato and this historians ought to remember. Whenever or wherever the potato is much talked of, hunger is stalking abroad"

These Red Cross food parcels were supposed to be exempt from examination as, under an international agreement, which the Germans had claimed to respect, guarantees had been given that they would never be used for any other purpose than the supply of supplementary food for prisoners-of-war. The parcels were compact and contained a well-balanced variety of tinned and other foods, including what was nectar to us – a 12-ounce. tin of condensed milk. Previously, I could never have imagined that my day would be made by just one teaspoonful of this gorgeous, thick, luscious liquid; and that if only I could restrain myself there would be another one tomorrow. There rarely was. Restraint became a very real problem, more especially with the five-day loaf. Some would eat half a loaf in a day; go without the following day; eat the other half the next day and so have nothing left for another two days. There seemed to be all sorts of ways to eke out a loaf, and certain people became known according to their habits as either 'hoarders' or 'bashers.'

Sometimes there was no choice because on a number of occasions the parcels had to pass through the hands of some exceptionally unpleasant Germans, who would insist on opening every packet and emptying out every tin. In the absence of containers, everything would be mixed together and shovelled back into the largest tin. No way could the contents be then kept for more than a day or so during summer months. We never came to know whether this breach of an agreement with the International Red Cross was the result of genuine suspicions regarding the contents of these parcels or just sheer bloody-mindedness. We had little doubt it was the latter.

It was soon learnt that we were allowed to receive parcels of clothing, books and other necessities up to ten pounds in weight. The first came for me a month or so before Christmas 1940, and I cannot have ever welcomed a change of underwear more. Also included were a few paperback books and some playing cards, the latter being especially popular. Every parcel was closely examined by the German authorities, who would take away any books almost automatically for further scrutiny. They also took away almost anything else that occurred to them. Some of the examiners were moderately friendly, whilst others would act like some crazed Customs Officer taking hours to search out every possibility of forbidden articles being cunningly hidden amongst innocent looking items. One such examiner in a display of excessive zeal and persevering thoroughness for which their race is renowned, decided to squeeze all the toothpaste out of its tube. What was left of your parcel to take back to your room would depend entirely on what sort of examiner it had been your luck to encounter. Some confiscated items were later returned but many others were never seen again.

Germany had signed the Geneva Convention, an international agreement on a code of conduct for the treatment of prisoners-of-war, one clause of which excluded officers from being made to do manual work. Other main clauses stated that a prisoner-of-war should be given two meals a day; a bed; facilities for washing and for exercise. It was also agreed that he could be kept a prisoner until the end of hostilities – a marked change from the Napoleonic wars, when many prisoners-of-war were returned to the countries they came from not long after their capture. In addition, neutral countries were to be assigned to opposing combatants to ensure that the terms of the Convention were being observed. On the whole, but with far too many glaring exceptions, the German army made at least some effort to respect the agreement for most of the war. However, the Gestapo, clearly regarded themselves to be far superior to all the armed forces and consequently felt themselves under no such obligation. We had not yet come across the plain-clothed Gestapo, but were destined to do so later. When we did, the friction between them and the army was very noticeable.

Sleep and dreams

With the arrival of personal parcels and books we had a new means of occupying ourselves and so there was a decline in the number of talks, which we had so welcomed and which had provided so much interest during a difficult period. There was, however, one more fascinating talk to come – entitled 'Dreams'.

Life in a German prison-of-war camp, from The Illustrated London News, April 1941

In his 'In Praise of Sleep' a seventeenth century author had written: "For do but consider what an excellent thing sleep is; it is so inestimable a jewel, that, if a tyrant would give his crown for an hour's slumber, it cannot be bought... for sleep is that golden chain that ties health and bodies together. Who complains of want, of wounds, of cares, of great men's oppressions, of captivity, whilst he sleepeth?"

The speaker expounded to us how our individual personalities affected our dreams, but how through undergoing common experiences in the camp our dreams were likely to reveal some common factors. Had anyone dreamt that he was sitting down to a hearty meal – steak perhaps, with all the trimmings - maybe wine? Several hands were raised. Had anyone dreamt of being chased yet escaping? Yes, again. These and other dreams of desire, as he termed them, were yet further ways in which nature was compensating for the situation we were in. It would, however, be indelicate to pursue this theme any further.

The talk ended with another quotation – from Thomas Nashe's "Terrors of the Night," written in 1593. "A dream is nothing else but a bubbling scum of froth of the fancy which the day has left undigested; ... In the daytime we torment our thoughts and imaginations with sundry cares and devices; at the night time they quake and tremble after the terror of their late suffering, and still continue thinking of the perplexities they have endured... Even as one's eyes glimmer and dazzle when they are withdrawn out of the light into darkness, so are our thoughts troubled and vexed when they are retired from labour to ease, and from skirmishing to surgery. You must give a wounded man leave to groan while he is in dressing; dreaming is no other than groaning while sleep, our surgeon,, hath us in his cure." Dreams, for most of us anyway, were clearly on the plus side of our restricted lives.

Currencies

One of the other plusses, especially for me, was the fact that I had never had any serious inclination to smoke cigarettes. Like many others I had tried them at school, and later, but had derived no particular pleasure from them; so for me anyway it wasn't something I had had to struggle to give up but, rather, a habit I had never developed. Whilst in Germany I came to enjoy smoking a pipe, and after the end of the war learnt to appreciate cigars. The regular smokers amongst us hadn't had a sniff of a cigarette for several months and were craving for them. So when eventually a small batch of Polish cigarettes suddenly arrived one day, and were shared out to smokers and non-smokers alike, I had no hesitation in giving my allocation to the first smoker who asked me for them.

This happy state of affairs for the smokers was not destined to last long because when the next batch arrived some weeks later, some of the more astute non-smokers had already come to realise that the humble cigarette had a value. It could be traded. Even those who were regarded as having the highest moral standards were not above this form of dealing. Whatever any of our principles might have been, this was but the beginning of an internal economy that had developed over the years as the cigarette rapidly became the only accepted unit of currency. In these early days cigarettes began to be exchanged for bread, or indeed any food, or even any possession. Understandably the smokers were outraged and thought it monstrous that non-smokers should stoop so low as to take advantage, as they saw it, of their addiction. There was, however, no contending with what I suppose we should now term market forces, nor indeed with human nature.

I had no inkling until then of the enormous craving that could overwhelm a cigarette smoker. At the massacre near Wormhout, it was reported, one of the first five soldiers to be lined up had asked permission for "a last cigarette" before being shot in the head. His request was refused. Similar requests have been recorded over the years from those about to be executed. What was it, I wondered,

Prisoner-of-war currency.

about a cigarette that anyone should choose it as a final solace before sudden death? Here in a prisoner-of-war camp the same craving was driving some smokers to sacrifice even what little food they had in order to indulge this pleasure. Reflecting on this one day I wondered how I could possibly accept food from a fellow officer who needed it as much as I did in exchange for something I didn't want and didn't even like. I have to confess I felt a bit of a cad, but was quick to discover that there were any number of other cads too. Another month or so and all scruples had been successfully buried. The cigarette was the established currency, and we began to enjoy our unexpected good fortune, though I cannot recall that it amounted to anything very much.

The only other currency was the specially printed German prisoner-of-war paper money with which we were paid at varying intervals. This money had virtually no value in Germany because there were few, if any, opportunities to buy anything with it. We were given to understand that it would eventually have an exchange value in England; that is if we ever returned home, and if the government of the day was in any position to exchange it. Consequently, for most of us it wasn't taken very seriously. It was an enlightening experience to live for several years in a community where one's own personal wealth, or lack of it, had virtually no meaning. Rich or poor, we all found ourselves in much the same financial situation.

Crimes and punishments

Whatever our rank, we all had to attend the twice-daily parades at which we were all counted. These tended to be rather tedious affairs as often the Germans would lose track and fail to reconcile their totals with the figures they had been given; then inevitably there would have to be a recount. "Eins, zwei, drei, vier, funf, sechs, sieben, acht, neun, zehn, .." We could hardly fail to learn how to count up to ten in German with this twice-daily repetition.

Very occasionally these parades provided some unexpected light relief. In the autumn of 1940 Alsatian dogs began to appear in the camp together with their handlers. The object was presumably to demonstrate that if any of us succeeded in escaping, we would be hunted down by these dogs that were clearly trained for just that purpose. It was therefore important to discover if they could be diverted from this prime function by being tempted with food – even titbits from the revolting meat sometimes found in the midday soup.

The Kommandant would usually appear on the morning parades accompanied by a diminutive Adjutant who spoke some English and who was charged with the duty of reading out camp orders. To do so he was obliged to stand on a wooden box to make himself seen. One morning he announced Camp Order No. 21: "It has come to the notice of the Kommandant that British officers have been giving meat to German dogs. This practice is forbidden. German dogs have been given instructions not to accept meat from British officers." Had we been parading inside, this order would have brought the roof down, but even in the open our laughter must have rung to the skies. The Kommandant looked embarrassed; his Adjutant closely examined his script to see if he had misread anything; and after a brief shrug of his shoulders Camp Order No. 22 was announced: "For laughing at German officers all British officers will be restricted to bread and water for the next three days." Honour, we supposed, was satisfied.

A number of orders had been issued during the long trek into Germany, the main concern apparently being that any of us might skip off for a romp in the hay with a German woman en route - a highly unlikely prospect but one that seemed to haunt the minds of our captors. Even after being enclosed in the confines of our camp and with no women ever in sight, the same orders were repeated. "British officers are strictly forbidden to have sexual intercourse with German women." When such orders were repeated with no opportunity for them to be flouted, it led us to wonder whether they sprang from the German preoccupation with the purity of their Teutonic race or whether they were just some sort of sadistic reminders that we were destined to remain in our celibate state for years to come.

The morning parade was also the occasion for announcing various punishments for those who had disobeyed the rules or who had committed some heinous offence such as escaping, or even attempting to do so. Retribution came in the form of so many days in the 'cooler', which meant solitary confinement. Some of these announcements brightened our day no end, such as the following examples:

"Awarded 5 days s.c. because he sat down on a stool to read whilst standing to attention."
"Awarded 8 days s.c. He was found to be writing P.O.W on the coat of a German who had put it down."
"Awarded 5 days s.c. because on morning parade, he behaved undisciplined blowing his nose in a provoking manner."
 "Awarded 8 days s.c. because when on morning parade he is knitting when all is standing to attention."
"Awarded 8 days s.c. because as a room senior he allowed the opening up of a hole without permission of the camp authorities."

Many ways to escape

'Opening up of holes' and other such activities became virtually the norm because it is the duty of a prisoner-of- war to make what attempts he can to escape. A close look at he massive barbed wire fence encircling the boundary of the camp and the numerous armed guards who made their presence felt day and night made any such thoughts seemingly impossible. Yet in this camp, as indeed in all the others I ever went to, some did manage to escape. The two most popular methods were either by tunnelling, a long laborious undertaking, or by brazen-faced bluff.

Three of us were confident that from such materials as we could muster, we could make a passable copy of a German officer's cap, which, if accepted might form at least part of a more elaborate uniform, which in turn could enable one of us to get out by bluffing his way through the main gate. This idea had a certain appeal if only because of the amount of work involved would entail much less hard labour than the rigours of tunnelling. It was perhaps just a dream, a bit of wishful thinking, although in fact some two years later it was used successfully in another camp. Anyway, we sought permission to go ahead from the Escape Committee, which had been set up to co-ordinate and approve any such attempts.

"Yes," said the officer in charge, "but none of you three will be the ones to make the attempt." "Why not?" we asked, "It's our idea." "Yes, but you must understand that as each attempt to escape is made, whether successful or not, it will be closely examined by the enemy who will relay the results of their findings to other camps all over Germany; each loophole in their security measures will be blocked and it will become increasingly difficult for anyone to escape at all. Furthermore," he added, "only the few who can speak fluent German will be given the chance anyway".

We felt he really didn't have to deliver the final blow to our hopes, but he did and it was the most shattering of them all. "What's more," he continued, "We need to concentrate all our efforts on those officers – almost certainly Regulars rather than Territorials – who are likely to be of the most use if they succeed in getting back to England, such as those who have been involved in Intelligence work." Having cut us down to size, he changed to a more conciliatory tone. "Now don't get depressed," he went on, "there are things you can do to help others to escape. Can you pick locks?" This question was put in a most matter of fact way as though he assumed that such an activity would naturally be part of whatever civilian occupation we might have embraced. "No?" he said, with an element of surprise in his voice, "Then are you any good at calligraphy? There are all sort of essential documents to be forged." He gave us the impression that any pre-war occupation might well have included forgery too, and was clearly pleased when I told him of my interest in calligraphy. I don't really know why but the idea of forgery was exciting and won instant appeal. Maybe I harboured the vague thought in the back of my mind that it might come in useful one day if we ever made it home to England.

The first task I was set, which I presumed to be some sort of test of ability, had very little to do with calligraphy because it involved the cutting out from an india rubber an exact copy of a censor's stamp. It had to be done with a razor blade and in reverse. The work was very much more difficult than I had imagined because it

Forged censor stamp

also had to be done in German lettering. When finished, a pad of moistened cloth impregnated with shavings from an indelible pencil made a passable impression that could be used on any document. At whatever stage had been reached, the rubber had to be concealed to avoid discovery in any of the frequent searches that punctuated our lives. It also required an enormous amount of patience, particularly because materials were scarce and couldn't be wasted.

The main purpose of this exercise was to enable any of us to imprint a copy of a German censor's stamp in books that had somehow missed being stamped by the censor, and also on papers, such as our own writings, which would otherwise risk being taken away if discovered during a search. When I eventually submitted my first effort to the Escape Committee, I was reminded of my school reports, which from time to time would include the words: "Could do better if he tried". However, I received some encouraging remarks and was told that it wasn't bad but I should have to do it again. My second effort, months later, was accepted.

Having become rather bored with the tedium of this particular task, I turned my attention to some of the other ancillary work that was deemed to be within the capabilities of Territorials such as most of us were. Watchers, or 'lookouts', were always wanted but on the whole 'stooges' as we were called, found the job rather boring, though it could be dangerous. On one occasion an officer who was sitting at a second floor window innocently painting, was regarded with suspicion by an alert sentry, who may have assumed he was one of our 'lookouts'. He shouted at him to move away. Not understanding, the officer remained where he was and was immediately shot in the head. This death came as a sharp reminder about who was in charge, and as a warning that the guards at that time who consisted mainly of troops resting from the front line, could indeed be alarmingly trigger-happy.

I longed to get down to actual forgery but the very fine nibs required were in extremely short supply and it was some time before I could acquire even one. Consequently it was some months before I was able to amass the necessary equipment and so start work which proved to be utterly fascinating. Meanwhile it was back to manual work helping out in the popular pastime – digging tunnels.

I very quickly realised this was not my forte. Maybe I was just too large to squeeze into narrow spaces, and I abhorred the fetid atmosphere and, even more so, working face down on my stomach. The best and most efficient moles were the smaller amongst us. The soil they extracted with such extraordinary and prolonged effort had to be 'lost,' and that involved yet another task which – like forgery – I was beginning to accept as one of the most natural things one would be expected to do the moment one signed up for the army. We would be given small bags of earth and on our perambulations around the exercise area we had to drop the earth down our trouser legs, spreading it far and wide whilst fully aware that sentries might be watching. Even a small tunnel would require the disposal of over twenty tons of earth and stone; and the fact that his amount from even one tunnel could be 'lost' successfully was a credit to the resourcefulness and ingenuity of those who toiled with such outstanding determination to achieve their goal. In winter, when there was snow about, the earth had to be put into the roof space, but mostly it was somehow dispersed around the camp grounds. A very considerable amount of earth must have been disposed of in this and other ways, yet the Germans never showed any signs of finding out what we had done with it.

Occasionally a tunnel would be discovered. Whenever this happened the whole camp could hardly fail to sense the sudden atmosphere of German joy. One day this led to another classic Camp Order: "You British officers think you can escape by digging tunnels. Well, we have found one! You think we know nothing, but we know damn all!" Another three days on bread and water, but it was worth it.

Inevitably there followed intensive searches; everything being torn apart that could be. Sometimes we would be kept waiting for five hours or so in the snow before being allowed back into our rooms, where we were confronted with a scene of utter devastation. Order would eventually be restored and we would scratch around for something to eat.

In November 1940 we were provided with enough musical instruments, including a grand piano, to form the basis of an orchestra. After much practice a concert was arranged, which included a variety of works, one being Schubert's Unfinished Symphony. The concert was attended by the Kommandant and his Adjutant. Fortunately, as the symphony was a fairly noisy piece, they couldn't hear the scratching sound made by the diggers who were working flat out – literally – several feet below the piano. The diggers were obliged to have someone on hand who could follow the music and so warn them of any quiet passages, during which they would cease to work abruptly, only to resume with renewed vigour as soon as louder music returned. They were probably the first diggers who ever dug to music.

That first concert may not have been very expert but it was truly wonderful to be able to listen to it. It made me realise for the first time how much good music, especially live performances, can be missed; and how easily it can be to take for granted the opportunity in normal life to be able to attend a concert. Denial of such opportunities over a lengthy period led to an actual longing or hunger for the sort of music that is worthy of one's full attention; music that is listened to rather than just heard. I also came to appreciate that music could have a spiritual value.

Many faiths

Most of us were self-styled 'Church of England', and those who practised their faith at all used to attend the C of E service on Sunday. Sometimes, though, there would be a Church of Scotland or possibly Methodist, Baptist or some other non-conformist Service. Most of these I attended at some time or other if only out of curiosity. The Church of Scotland Service was unusual in that

OFLAG VIIc, LAUFEN

FORT XV THORN. POLAND
STALAG XX A.
1941

THORN REPRISAL CAMP

ARB

LAUFEN, VIIc

© HARRINGTON

'YES, I QUITE GAVE UP CUNARD AFTER THEY ASKED ME TO SHARE A CABIN'

instead of approaching the altar to receive Communion the congregation stayed where they were (this could have been a convenience just for us) whilst a small basket of little cubes of bread was passed around for us to help ourselves. I wondered if I was the only one to harbour the unworthy thought that if I was quick I might pick out one of the larger ones.

In those early days this variety of Services was possible because there were over forty padres of all denominations, who, to begin with, were all accommodated in one room together. Years later I came to reflect on what a heaven-sent opportunity this might have been to further the cause of Christian Unity; and how even today the confinement of dissenting Christian leaders in one place – and not too comfortable a one at that – until such time as they resolved their differences might well result in astonishing progress. After two months or so almost all our forty padres were dispersed amongst other camps throughout Germany, leaving us with one Church of England padre, one Presbyterian Minister and one Roman Catholic Chaplain. I never attended the latter's services, which I was told were all in Latin, as someone had warned me about getting involved with "all that mumbo-jumbo, and heaven only knows what goes on behind those closed doors!"

For what was probably the first time, I began to ponder about my own faith within the Church of England; the faith in which I had been brought up. My thoughts were not concerned so much with the only Church I had known until then as with why anyone should think differently. What was it that had convinced those who were not within the Established Church to dissent from it to the extent of adopting permanently for themselves another label? Curiosity had been aroused and in that winter of 1940 were sown the seeds of a deepening interest in what actually divided the various Christian faiths. It was two years before I came to think more seriously about it again.

The world beyond the camp…

Meanwhile Christmas had come and gone without any noticeable difference in our daily routine. The start of the New Year of 1941 inspired fresh thinking; less preoccupation with ourselves and more concern about what might be going on in the rest of the world. There was little hope of gathering any accurate summary of the situation, as the only news that came our way was trough the German papers, which, naturally to us, continued to present dismal reading. We had already learnt that Italy had sided with Germany and had declared war on Britain and France on 10th June 1940. We also learnt that Russia had signed a pact with Germany. We had no means of knowing for certain that Germany had in a matter of three weeks completely routed the armies of France. Nor were we to know then that the British army had only been saved from annihilation by the extraordinary successful evacuation from Dunkirk. Since these disastrous events Britain had stood alone facing a victorious Germany and Italy, having lost thousands of men and an enormous amount of armour and equipment. To most of the world it must have appeared that the war was virtually over and all that remained was for the vultures to swoop down for pickings.

At this crucial time we had no knowledge either of the famous 'Battle of Britain', which was to have such a significant effect upon any possible decision by Hitler regarding the invasion of England. I think many of us assumed there would be such an invasion, and expected news of it to be splashed across the German papers at any time. But it never appeared. Instead there was any amount of coverage of the intensive bombing of London and other cities, with exaggerated accounts of damage done and the negligible losses of German aircraft compared with the huge British losses.

I sometimes wonder if any of us fully realised just how serious the situation really was during the latter half of 1940, both for our country and for ourselves. We could only imagine the devastating effects the continuous bombing of our cities had on the people in them, and more especially on our own relatives and friends. For us, if Germany had then conquered Britain, there would have been little to look forward to beyond labour camps for an indefinite period, or worse.

In this New Year of 1941, we were to be rudely shaken out of any further gloomy speculation about the conduct of the war by an unexpected and rather more immediate concern for ourselves. Early in March we experienced the first of four reprisals, which involved the departure of some five hundred of the younger officers, including myself. We were accompanied by a few senior officers, amongst whom was the Commander-in-Chief of the 51st Highland Division, which had been captured almost en bloc at St, Valery on the northern coast of France – Major-General Sir Victor Fortune – who was an inspiration to us all. Our destination was to be Poland.

PART FOUR
Poland

"Misery acquaints a man with strange bedfellows"
The Tempest, II, 2

REPRISALS were acts of retaliation by Germany for the alleged maltreatment of their own prisoners-of-war in British hands. The decision to retaliate at all was political rather than military and the first consequence of this, which quickly became very apparent to us all, was how powerless we were to do anything about it, and how we were no more than pawns in the political arena.

The reason for this move to Poland, we were told, would be explained to us on arrival there. Meanwhile, gathering together the meagre possessions each of us had acquired, we left Oflag VIIC on our way to a train, in which we were to spend three wretched days and two nights before eventually arriving at Poznan in the centre of Poland.

Poznan camp

That evening, sore from the long hard journey, cold and certainly hungry, we could see immediately that we were in for trouble. The arc lights at the station revealed the welcoming party – a long row of guards with their rifles at the ready, safety catches off and fingers on the triggers, and behind them another, shorter, row with machine guns aimed straight at us. We were formed up into groups of a hundred, five abreast, because all the counting was always done in fives. After the actual count and inevitable re-count had taken place, we were ready to move off.

In the gathering gloom, what seemed like battalions of guards, some of whom were handling dogs, lined up on either side of us. At last we were about to move off but not until a number of mounted guards, who trotted up and down the column wielding long horse-whips, had played their part too in this show of strength. The order was finally given and we set off to trudge through the streets on the outskirts of the town, and an armoured tank suddenly emerged from the darkness of the trees to rumble along behind us.

In all the years I can recall as a prisoner-of-war, this was the lowest point that was ever reached and the most humiliating. It was probably fully intended to be so in order to impress the silent Poles who watched us pass by. What they saw were hundreds of dishevelled British officers clutching their belongings being shouted at,

Fortress at Poznan, Stalag XXI, D. British prisoners were sent to Poznan as a "reprisal" for alleged maltreatment of German prisoners in Canada.

some being prodded, and some actually kicked as they were herded like cattle through a part of the town and on to an exceedingly muddy track stretching for nearly a mile.

When we were finally assembled at the entrance of the underground fortress, which was to be our new camp, we were harangued by the Kommandant, who informed us that we were there as a reprisal for the way in which the British army were treating German prisoners-of-war in Fort Henry in Canada. Until this treatment ceased, we were to undergo the same conditions as they were being subjected to. We would be overcrowded; be given a minimum of light and be locked in our rooms all night. He went on listing more retributions but we weren't listening. What did it matter any further? That whole evening since our arrival at the station was so fantastic in its theatrical display of the less attractive aspects of the German character, with its preoccupation with dominance and power, that many of us now experienced a sense of comic relief. We continued to stand there wondering what else the Kommandant could come up with to make our stay there more wretched. He had nearly finished, and was now raising his voice to tell us that he had good news for us as well. We were to be granted immediately an extra postcard to enable us to write home to our MPs, urging them to use their influence to ensure conditions changed in Fort Henry so that this reprisal could be ended. Sad to relate, I was told that one officer actually did this.

The fortress itself was mainly below ground level, with about a fifth of it above the surface. It was surrounded by a large empty moat and looked every inch a prison. To reach our rooms on the lowest level, we had to descend two flights of stone stairs accompanied by guards with rubber truncheons. The noise we made sent rats scurrying away. Our room contained five wooden beds, each constructed to take six men – three up and three down. There was a single feeble electric light in the centre of the ceiling, and the only window that looked out on the rather grim moat had been meticulously boarded up three-quarters of the way, because "that's all the light permitted to German prisoners in Canada".

The damp and smell that pervaded these lower rooms came mainly from an underground pipe, which, presumably, leaked somewhere. Most likely it was where the rats lived and bred. But they weren't the only signs of wildlife – there were also fleas, hundreds of them. We even used to amuse ourselves by trying to catch them, and from time to time would organise competitions with neighbouring rooms to see who could catch the most in a given period. It was curious that some would be covered in bites whereas other failed to suffer even one. The old theory that fleas were only attracted by alcohol in the blood, or maybe the absence of it, just didn't apply because none of us had tasted alcohol for many months.

On the first evening we were to encounter more wildlife, this time in the form of lice and bed bugs. In the absence of any antidote, there was little we could do about them other than try and keep ourselves as clean as possible, which wasn't made easy by the water never being much more than one degree above freezing. Personal hygiene was a major problem and the toilet facilities were primitive to a degree almost beyond belief.

Whatever the weather, we had to parade on the grassy roof twice a day for the endless counting routine and were duly locked in our rooms at 8.00 pm until 7.30 am on the following day. The room was just large enough to accommodate the five rickety beds plus one small table, leaving virtually no space in which to move around. The palliasses on which we spent many a restless night were partially filled with a mixture of wood shavings and straw leaving plenty of room for the fleas, lice and bed bugs. We were thoughtfully provided with two open buckets for the natural and nocturnal needs of the thirty of us for the eleven and a half hours of our confinement. It was hard to believe that the British were subjecting German prisoners-of-war to similar conditions in Canada but we were never to find out. In these dreary circumstances it was timely to count one's blessings. One for which we were mightily thankful was that none of the thirty in our room fell ill or suffered from diarrhoea.

Escaping from this fortress was exceptionally difficult although there was one triumphant effort in which the two officers concerned somehow managed to get themselves to Switzerland. Another two officers, who were being taken out to a dentist in the town, made a less successful attempt. They may have been spurred on by the dread of an old-fashioned drill, no anaesthetics and only cement for fillings, or perhaps the thought of having to return to the fortress was too much for them; anyway, they managed to give their guards the slip. Unfortunately for them, their freedom was very short-lived and they were both back again the following day, but their guards were never seen again.

A Radio!

There was no knowing how long this reprisal was going to last, so we just had to make the best of it, consoled by the thought that at least things couldn't get any worse. As so often happens at such times there was indeed a glimmer of light. We had not been slow to recognise the potential advantage of being in a friendly country. Within a few weeks Polish workmen, who were made to do various menial tasks in the fortress, succeeded in smuggling in the component parts of a radio, which electronic experts amongst us were able to assemble. Unexpectedly, then, we found ourselves with a radio, which had to be dismantled every evening and the various parts dispersed around for safe hiding; it then had to be reassembled each day in time for the BBC broadcast. Thus it was possible for the first time to hear news from our own side about the conduct of the war. Our own security surrounding the set was very strict and only a few ever knew where it was, and only two, so I was told, actually listened to the broadcasts, which were always introduced by the opening bars of Beethoven's Fifth Symphony with its…-, the Morse Code V for Victory.

All enemy propaganda was notoriously unreliable, and very probably the news as announced by the BBC's Overseas Services was not entirely free from some sort of propaganda either, more especially as it was directed to our allies in Europe, to whom it was a great encouragement. It also embodied a number of coded messages which were of enormous help to the thousands of men and women risking their lives and those of their families in the various resistance movements particularly in France, Belgium and Holland.

Until the time of this reprisal in Poland the only news we had been able to come by had been gathered from the German papers, which the camp authorities were keen for us to read. For the most part they were still full of what appeared to be endless German successes in almost every direction. The acquisition of our clandestine radio came as an enormous relief from this surfeit of enemy propaganda and was a great morale booster. Morale reached even greater heights when we heard the astounding news, on the very day after it happened that Hitler's Deputy, Rudolf Hess, had flown to Scotland. From that time we were never without a radio. The set, or, rather, sets, survived snap searches and even more remarkably, the very thorough searches that always took place on departure and again on arrival at another camp. They also survived the detection devices that were later employed in an effort to pinpoint their whereabouts. The ingenuity with which this was so successfully accomplished for so long a period was truly outstanding, and those who were not directly involved were ever grateful to those who were, even though their names were never known to us.

The world beyond the camp...

We could see from the roof of the fortress a railway line in the distance, and, day after day, wagons laden with tanks on their way east. Germany was clearly preparing either to defend her borders or more likely, we thought, to invade Russia. How right we were! The Non-Aggression Pact which Hitler had signed with Russia in August 1939 was breached in the most dramatic way in the summer of 1941, when Germany launched a blistering attack on the longest possible front stretching from the Baltic to the Black Sea. This treachery thus made Russia our ally in the struggle against the Nazis. What appeared at the time to be good news was especially welcome after so many depressing reports about the heavy air raids on Britain; the disasters in the Balkans and Greece followed by the loss of Crete. The so-called good news about our new ally was soon to be dashed by later news, which talked of the rapid advance into Russian territory by German forces, who, it seemed, were carrying all before them. This advance was so successful that German forces could have taken Moscow if they hadn't been diverted, on Hitler's personal orders, to Leningrad.

Torun camp

For us, the only cheer amidst the gloom was the lifting of the reprisal we were under, without any explanation. After three months at Poznan it appeared that the conditions at Fort Henry must have improved because half our number were moved to another underground fortress some eighty miles still further east, at Torun (Thorn). The only real difference was relief from the over-crowding, which had become very oppressive. Even at Torun, whilst not exactly overcrowded, a great deal of patience was still required to live week after week in such unnecessary proximity to each other. One could hardly fail to be aware of every little quirk of character; strengths and weaknesses; the extent to which each bothered to keep himself clean; what amused him and what didn't. The list could go on and on. There was very little chance of hiding anything about oneself, even if one wanted to. Human nature in the raw and under duress tends to reveal, probably quite subconsciously, the depths that psychologists tell us we all have. Yet in spite of everything I can not recall a single incident that led to any physical violence. Arguments raged from time to time, and could get quite heated but always stopped short of any real ill feeling. I don't know if this was the experience of others but it was certainly mine. It was impossible not to learn a great deal about human nature, and indeed about oneself – perhaps the most valuable experience of all.

The Kommandant at Torun (Thorn) was more relaxed about the conditions we were supposed to be living under, and the last remnants of the reprisal gradually petered out. The fortress itself was just as squalid as the one at Poznan and was also mainly underground. The one window in our room was not boarded up, nor were we locked in our rooms at night, but there was no lack of either rats or fleas. At last, after nearly five months, the reprisal came to an end and we were moved to a very different camp much further south.

BACK TO GERMANY

Southern Germany camp

In sharp contrast to the dreary landscape of Poland, there was now the welcoming sight, though far away, of the snow-capped mountains of neutral Switzerland. We were once again in southern Germany. The Kommandant, an unusually cheerful character, addressed us all on our first parade in words to this effect: "Some of you, as we well know, are going to think about escaping from here so I would urge you to think again. Whatever schemes you British officers may come up with, remember this – we Germans know them all. This camp is heavily guarded and any of you who attempt to escape thinking you are playing some sort of game with us will soon find it is no game at all. The sentries have orders to shoot. Escaping is no longer a sport."

It became clear much later that the reason for our unusually short stay in this camp, only six months, was that the lure of Switzerland in fact led to more actual and attempted escapes than ever. As, apparently no Escape Committee had been formed, we assumed it was a free-for-all and very shortly I became involved, with nineteen others, in a tunnel. I was spared the task of the digging as this, thankfully, was left to those of smaller stature. There were plenty of other jobs to be done and I found the days filled with the already familiar routine of soil disposal; the creation from sundry materials of 'civilian' clothes; the ever present need for 'lookouts' and the general organisation needed for 'going away.' We all looked upon this venture more as a welcome diversion, a bit of fun, to add some stimulation to our lacklustre lives, and who was to know – we might actually make it.

It was very important to ensure a higher standard of physical fitness, so exercise was stepped up and we all started to walk much further each day and to take part in whatever physical training was being organised. Two weeks before we were due to get out, the leader of our group scrambled to the end of the tunnel and thrust a stick up through the grass at the point where we were hoping to emerge – some yards well beyond the perimeter wire – whilst a lookout watched for it from a vantage point within the camp. Up went the stick, very difficult to spot at a distance of over a hundred feet, but although just outside it was too close to the wire and so more digging was required. We were elated at the progress we had made and were eagerly looking forward to the actual attempt, the timing of which had to coincide with the absence of a moon. We had even fixed the order in which we were to go through the tunnel. Preference was given to the smaller of us as they would get through more quickly whereas the larger of us would run the danger of becoming jammed in such a tight space or even causing it to collapse. I was allotted the eleventh place in the order. However, whilst this finishing work was being completed, I began to experience acute abdominal pains and had to report to the doctor, whose immediate diagnosis was appendicitis.

Just before being whisked away in an ambulance, I was seen by our tunnel leader who, whilst commiserating with my misfortune, was clearly much more concerned with the risk that under anaesthetic I might blurt out something to do with our activities. I was therefore instructed to "control yourself at all times; stay awake as long as possible, (whatever that meant) and keep alert, especially when coming round from the operation". I assured him that I would do my best.

I was taken outside the camp to a small room in a Convent run by an Order of nuns; prepared for the operation and taken to the theatre the same day. As I lay on the operation table, the German surgeon injected my arm with (I think) Evipan and I was told to count aloud and that I would reach about twelve before losing consciousness. I started to count. With some alarm I passed twenty and still feeling wide-awake several uncomfortable thoughts occurred to me simultaneously. My urgent instructions just before leaving the camp were to stay awake as long as possible, a prospect that had minimum appeal at that moment. Then there was the dreadful thought that the surgeon might lose patience – I was after all only an expendable prisoner – and start his work even if I went on counting. The sheer horror of these thoughts came to an end, so I was told later, just as I reached twenty-seven.

I awoke in a comfortable bed in a room on the ground floor of the Convent with its window barred on the outside, and a nun brought me food. The following morning the surgeon, a Major in uniform, came into the room and extended his hand in greeting. I was happy to shake his hand, and tried to thank him for operating me. Neither he nor any of the nuns spoke any English, so it was particularly difficult for him to ask me what appears to be an important question for those who have just had an appendix removed. He needed to know if I had passed wind; and he did his best to illustrate the question by puffing up his cheeks and blowing whilst at the same time pointing to his behind. My first thought was that he was suffering from flatulence, though why he should bother to convey this fact to me was a mystery. Eventually, however, the meaning got through to me and all was well.

The two days I spent in this Convent were unbelievable bliss. I had a bed of my own, sheets, peace and quiet, and the tender care of a nun who had no illusions about the Hitler regime. On the morning of my departure she brought me an egg for breakfast, something I hadn't seen for two years. She bent over me and whispered, "Hitler nix gut!"

On my return to the camp I was housed in the Infirmary for another week or so. Our doctor's final examination of my new scar, before returning me to the room I had left, confirmed his view that the operation had been carried out very efficiently indeed, the scar being very small. As a footnote to all this, I should add that twelve years later back in England I had another bout of abdominal pains and our GP was called. A brief examination, and he reached for the telephone to request a bed for an appendicitis case. I hastened to tell him there was just one problem – I had had it out. Slamming down the phone, he made a hasty re-examination, found the minute scar, made his excuses and left.

More ways to escape

While in the infirmary I learnt that three of our tunnel party had managed to escape just before the tunnel collapsed. They were all re-captured within a matter of hours. Back in my room, I was to hear of a friend whom I knew fairly well and who had managed to escape dressed as a young woman. Having rested overnight in a wood, he was obliged to cross a road. All seemed clear when suddenly a motorcycle screeched to a halt beside him and he was offered a lift. Unable to speak any German he bashfully signified his acceptance. Within seconds he found himself on the pillion seat clasping a German soldier around his waist and heading off at great speed into the distance. Unluckily, the brief journey proved disastrous for his disguise; not only did his wig blow off, but one of his 'boobs' became dislodged and fell out of his shirt on to the road. On arrival at a small village, his disguise had been blown, literally, and, to compensate for the frustration of any amorous intentions, the soldier recouped what credit he could for so successfully recapturing an escaped prisoner-of-war.

The many escapes from this camp were probably responsible for the haste with which we were moved once again, leaving behind us the usual network of tunnels. This time our journey was to take us to Warburg, a town some twenty miles north-west of Kassel in central Germany.

The world beyond the camp…

There was not much good news during 1941. In the early part of the year, the area of conflict was widened by the German conquest of Yugoslavia and then Greece. This in turn was followed by the fall of Crete, which resulted in the eventual influx of another batch of British prisoners-of-war to our various camps. The initial German onslaught into Russia had gone very well to begin with, but by the late summer was showing signs of faltering. Up until that time the enemy must have had every reason to feel on top of the world, but change was in the air.

In spite of enormous losses of merchant shipping to German U-boats in what came to be known as the Battle of the Atlantic, and in spite of suffering continual air bombardment, Britain was standing firm. No longer having to bear the brunt of the war against the Nazis entirely alone; and encouraged by the success against all odds in the air in the Battle of Britain in 1940, Britain was regrouping and strengthening her forces for eventual attack, but it would still be many months before any serious offensive could be mounted.

Some of these facts we knew and some we could only surmise, but such were our thoughts as we wended our way to Warburg.

Warburg camp

Apart from the original long trek into Germany, this was the fourth brief period of being in transit between camps. Spirits always seemed to rise on such occasion, maybe because the grass over the hill is always greener; maybe because, if even for a brief period, there was a welcome change of view from the endless stretches of barbed wire; or, though still under heavy guard there was a hint of a freedom to come, together with a sudden relief from being confined in a cage. On the physical level, constriction for a long time can lead to similar constriction in the mind; to too much introspection; to too much preoccupation with personal well being and to being ensnared in a little private world.

The grass over the hill was anything but greener. Oflag VÎB at Warburg was unforgettable mainly because of its most vexatious

Sketch of Warburg Camp, Oflag VII b.

Search at Warburg Camp, from 'Joe in Germany' by Jimmy Graham and Jack Thomas, printed by Surey Fine Art Press, 1946.

characteristics. There was mud everywhere, which seemed to get into every corner of the rooms. The wooden huts were penetrated by every icy wind and, indeed, ice would form on the inside of the thinly slatted walls. The single stoves gave forth a minimum of grudging heat; and carbide lamps provided the only lighting if and when carbide happened to be available. These lamps hissed out an eerie glow, which was reckoned to be bad for the eyes, although it could be just bright enough to read by. On top of all this the Kommanditur comprised some of the most unpleasant German staff we had yet encountered.

'Hoarders and bashers'

Snap searches, and there were many, would start at dawn and we would often be kept outside in bitter weather for six or seven hours. During this time, and from a study of methods employed, it appeared that the discovery of forbidden articles was of secondary importance. The main object was the wholesale destruction of personal articles, with Red Cross food being the main target. Sometimes parcels from the Red Cross would include a bar of chocolate – a luxury for us, and presumably for the senders too – but even more so for the enemy searchers, who probably hadn't seen it for years. Why should their prisoners be allowed such a wartime delicacy whilst they and their families went without? The temptation to grab it in such a heaven-sent opportunity often proved too great. When the search was over those considered as 'hoarders,' would sometimes find that the chocolate they had so carefully hidden in their palliasses or elsewhere was missing. Thus, most of the 'hoarders' became instant converts to 'bashers'. At one camp where this happened the Senior British Officer reported the loss to the camp Kommandant, who took the complaint seriously. It was, he said, a slur upon the German army and would be investigated. A few days later it was reported back that the culprit had been discovered and had been dealt with, but that the chocolate couldn't be returned. It had, presumably, been eaten.

In this third year of the war it surprised us that such items as chocolate were still available in England, and we began to get concerned about what sacrifices were being made at home in order to send us any at all. It came to light much later that German prisoners-of-war in British hands also received some similar wartime luxuries not generally available in Germany at the time. On either side it was most likely a genuine effort to send some special cheer to relatives in enemy hands, but it may also have been intended to convey a political message to the enemy searchers that their respective countries were a long way from starvation.

Health problems, physical and mental

It was during the latter half of the long winter of 1941 and 1942 that some of us began to reveal signs of more serious health problems in both body and mind. We had then been in Germany for almost two yeas and time was beginning to take its toll. A fellow officer in my regiment contracted meningitis, and as there were no essential drugs available he died. I had a recurrence of asthma attacks, which I used to have as a child, but there was nothing to be done about it as there were no remedies to hand. Anyone who has ever experienced a bad attack in such circumstances will know how frightening it can be. Luckily these attacks ceased after a while and they never recurred.

One officer must have, temporarily anyway, taken leave of his senses because apparently not being able to stand captivity any longer he ran to the perimeter and started to climb up the barbed wire with his bare hands in broad daylight. He was promptly shot.

ABORT ADJOINING WASHOUSE AT END OF BLOCK
EASTERN SQUATTER TYPE INFESTED WITH.
BUGS, RATS, FLEAS, FLIES AND SMELLS. GRAHAM 44.

The wash-house.

89

I came to hear years later of a similar incident that occurred in another camp and how the body there was left clinging to the barbed wire fence for three days as a grim warning to others.

There were other signs of mental aberration, mostly very minor and we took little notice of them; even of the occasion when four of us were playing bridge and after a while whoever was 'dummy' left to go to the lavatory but didn't return. When we eventually found him, he had quite forgotten that he had been in the middle of a game. I recall that particular game very well because whilst playing a hand I completely lost track of what I was trying to achieve. I had been struck by the sudden thought: what on earth were we doing there anyway, playing Bridge? Had we forgotten there was a war on? Many of those we knew were out somewhere fighting; our families were being bombed and here we were playing cards! Totally incongruous and totally frustrating.

There were two or three others who were assumed to have 'got religion'. It was expressed as though they had caught some disease. One of these, a Maori officer, would occasionally regale us by singing a hymn in the middle of the night, and another would stay up all hours deep in audible prayer. Neither of these nocturnal devotions commended themselves to the rest of the room and they were gently yet firmly discouraged. Although these incidents were fairly rare, they proved to be rather unsettling and left a feeling of uneasiness that was difficult to define. We consoled ourselves with the thought that the war couldn't go on for much longer.

Another officer, who some also assumed to be round the bend, proclaimed during a discussion on what occupations we might take up on our return that he wanted to be a monk. At that time we had been in Germany for well over two years and this idea seemed to most of us just inconceivable. His name was Roberts and he later became the Abbot of Downside.

Whilst there were no sleepwalkers, which would have been a highly dangerous practice, there were one or two who occasionally talked in their sleep. One of them provided a particularly entertaining night, which I can vouch for, as I was one of several who heard him. At some unearthly hour in the morning, I was suddenly startled to hear from a bed nearby: "Seven no trumps!" and then in an equally clear tone: "Double – bubble." There followed a pause during which I was straining every nerve not to miss what might come next, and I wasn't disappointed. In a voice charged with emotion, the word "Redouble" was spat out with all the pent-up venom of a cobra. Sadly, that was all and the officer concerned didn't remember a thing about it when we asked him how he enjoyed his game of bridge the previous night.

The seemingly endless arguments about how long the war would go on were subdued for a while when someone had the bright idea of running a sweepstake on the actual day it would end. We now had the opportunity to back our opinions with our paper money and the winner, or winners, would be paid whatever meagre sums we were to pledge by way of prize money "when we get home." Of the two thousand or so in the camp most took part. The summary of the answers was indeed surprising. The vast majority selected that very year – 1942 – most choosing the date 11th November. Quite a number backed various dates in 1943; a few favoured some dates in 1944, and about six or so selected dates in 1945. These latter were assumed to be already round the bend. I never found out who won, nor if the winner was ever able to collect his winnings.

More escapes

The camp at Warburg was remarkable for the most brilliantly conceived, and executed, escape of the war. The plan, in essence, was to rush ladders up against the perimeter wire itself and, by means of a hinged plank at the top of the ladder, leap across the breadth of the barbed wire and jump down the other side. An enormous amount of planning was involved, which included the construction of the ladders and keeping them concealed. As the attempt was to be made at night it was vital that all the perimeter lights could be fused at the critical moment. To achieve this, underground cables had to be located, tunnels dug, and, at great risk, live cables cut. Sadly, one officer was electrocuted whilst in a tunnel attempting this vital work.

On the moonless night chosen for the escape, all the perimeter lights were successfully fused and even the searchlights were powerless whilst some twenty or so, with the help of the ladders, managed to surmount the wire fence. Shots were fired all over the camp, many bullets easily penetrating the flimsy wooden walls of our huts causing much confusion and consternation but, luckily no one was hurt. One of the escapees was caught immediately as he had broken his ankle in the jump down the other side of the wire. Most of the others were out for some hours; a few for several days, and just one succeeded in finding his way back to England, where he too eventually became a monk.

Mini – reprisals started almost immediately. We were all turned out early the following morning whilst a massive search took place for most of the day with the customary destruction of personal property. Outside in the icy winds it was certainly bitterly cold; but even inside the wooden huts with their flimsy walls it could often be almost as icy. Most of us would lie on our bunks at night under every vestige of clothing we could possibly find. It must have been during some of the bleakest weather in this camp that many of us had a first experience of that numbing cold that saps all physical energy and equally paralyses the mind. Parades lasted much longer than usual because the Germans seemed to keep getting their figures wrong. Whether this was just through incompetence or maybe contrived deliberately we couldn't be sure, but most of us suspected the latter.

Great escapes from German camps have been the subject of several post-war films, but there doesn't appear to have been one depicting this escape nor one other which is equally worth recording even though it involved only one officer.

One of the British orderlies, of whom there were some thirty in the camp, had been ordered to clean out one of the sentry boxes on the perimeter. Being very observant, he noticed that when looking towards the next sentry box there was an area halfway between the two where the coiled barbed wire appeared to be so thick that it constituted a blind spot. His report about this resulted in a brilliant escape by an officer sufficiently small in stature, who managed to cut through the coils of wire and, being sufficiently small in stature, wriggle his way to freedom, emerging successfully on the other side. To have any hope of achieving this aim, diversions had to be organised to attract and maintain the attention of the two sentries involved. Thus, in front of one sentry box, a group of officers started to fool around and at a given signal one managed to set light to his hair. This proved to be riveting entertainment for that sentry. At the same time I found myself amongst a group being watched by the other sentry, the centre of attraction being the well-known - even to the Germans – legless pilot Wing-Commander Bader, who had been persuaded to unscrew both his legs. These we tossed around to each other as though it was some sort of game. This sentry's attention was equally distracted for long enough to enable the escape to be made. When on the next parade it was discovered that there was one missing, the Germans went to endless trouble to find out how it had been achieved. They appeared to be completely baffled for over two days before they finally came to examine the wire more closely.

Shortly afterwards and without warning we were suddenly ordered to move camp once more, and this time our destination was to be an army barracks at Eichstaat in southern Germany, where we were destined to spend almost all of our remaining time.

The world beyond the camp…
This move, in September 1942, triggered off further thinking about momentous events that had been taken place way beyond our perimeters. During the month of December 1941, the Japanese had launched their surprise attack against American warships at Pearl Harbour, four days after which Germany declared war against the United States. The involvement of both the U.S.A and Japan left no doubt but that this was now truly a global war. Germany and Italy – the Axis – now had another ally in Japan, whilst Britain and Russia were joined by the U.S.A. It had been possible to learn of all these events through both the German papers and through our hidden radio; but there were many other events about which we couldn't possibly know at the time and maybe it was just as well. Foremost amongst these was the continuing slaughter of Jews within Germany itself and in all countries which were under its control. Thousands upon thousands of Jewish men, women and children, even babies, were herded day after day into waiting gas chambers. War spreads an ugly atmosphere which envelopes all those involved in it to the extent that the really dreadful things that happen in it come to be thought of as only to be expected. Years later it is difficult to believe that such atrocities actually took place, but they did; and the German extermination of the Jews was nothing short of mass murder on a scale that had never before been even imagined.

The first part of 1942 brought more depressing news about still further successes by the Germans in the Atlantic Sea and in the defeat of the Allies' Commando attack on Dieppe, with the loss of much valuable equipment and nearly two thousand Canadian prisoners. The war was going well too for the Japanese who were sweeping down Malaya, and had already taken Kuala Lumpur.

At the time of our move however, there were at least some indications that the tide was beginning to turn favour of the Allies.

It had taken three years to reach this point from what had started as a seemingly limited war fought by Britain and France against Nazi Germany. Now the war had extended beyond Europe to North Africa and the Far East. For those of us who had at that time been in Germany for nearly two and a half years, the rapid expansion of the war now involving millions of people all over the world had one particular disturbing effect. We were becoming increasingly remote from it, and there was an uncomfortable but growing realisation of our almost total irrelevance to it.

PART FIVE

Eichstaat . . . and Freedom

"The art of our necessities is strange
That can make vile things precious"
King Lear, III, 2

Another move – would the grass be greener over the hill this time? Indeed it was and our spirits were lifted at the first sight of the attractive valley in which the small town of Eichstaat was situated. In sharp contrast to the cheerless plains of Westphalia, which we had just left, our new camp presented us with a vista of pine forests and hilly countryside. Furthermore, the accommodation we were to occupy was solidly built and had electricity. Outside was a large playing ground, and there was also the prospect of a theatre. The main drawback, at least to begin with, was once again the German staff, most of whom gave an all too clear impression of being very committed Nazis.

Moving to another camp always disrupted the flow of the Red Cross food parcels on which we had come to depend. Until this flow was resumed we had to sustain ourselves on the standard diet of watery soup, the inevitable sauerkraut, turnips which seemed to have been made from plywood, bad potatoes and very occasionally klippfisch – a dried white fish with a most unsavoury smell.

In 1943 the unexpected arrival of a number of Canadian officers fresh from the disastrous raid on Dieppe stepped up our interest in the outside world. New faces in our midst were very welcome to us. Even before this event it was quite extraordinary how, taking one's daily walk, it was possible to come across someone one hadn't seen before. Enquiring further usually led to the inevitable answer that they had been with us all of our three years.

A study of faiths

During this time a large quantity of books had been accumulating and it was now possible to set up a library. Many of these books were classified as technical, and a separate section was found for them, which also included many books of reference. As with the main library, volunteers were needed to help with this section; to list and classify all the books and so to make it possible for anyone to borrow them on the lines of a normal library. I was very pleased to have been accepted to help in this work, which provided me with a particular interest almost every day for quite a long time. I cannot remember how, nor indeed when, but a photograph was

THE LIBRARY STAFF

(*Back Row*)—Richard Hunt (Law); Jim Hawkes (Architecture); Peter Moir (Technical); Ronny Ashford (Technical); Pet Verity (Technical); Dorriene Belson (Technical); Bob Currer (Engineering); Tommy Spiers (Technical); Brian Bell (Technical); Jack Tayler (Technical); Andrew Biggar (Agricultural).

(*Front Row*)—Arthur Fleet; John Buxton (Deputy Librarian—Technical); E. M. Viney; Duncan Ranking (Fiction); Tony Rothlea (Assistant Education Officer); Pat Heenan (Assistant Education Officer).

taken of the two library staff, which found its way into the December 1944 issue of Country Life magazine.

Amongst all these books were a number on the various religions of the world, and as I had already been curious about the beliefs that separated Christians, I suddenly found an unexpected opportunity to study almost any faith in as much detail as I wanted. I started with the main world religions but soon realised that this was far too big an undertaking, so decided to concentrate on Christianity.

Within the confines of a camp, and surrounded by fellow countrymen, the Church of England still seemed very relevant, but it was beginning to appear less so in the wider context of so many variations, about which I had such very limited knowledge. Apart from the various nonconformist churches, which were puzzling enough in themselves the C of E seemed to embrace its own divisions between Low and High Church, of which the latter was more familiar as I had been brought up as an Anglo-Catholic.

In a regimental army officer's mess religion was one of the subjects never mentioned. However, here in Germany, thrown together in one vast officers' mess, the situation was very different. Maybe because of the dramatic events that had happened to each one of us, both before and after we had become prisoners-of-war, we were already adopting a more flexible attitude to life generally.

" BOOK " STAFF (DEALING WITH PARCELS)

(Back Row)—Donald Jackson (Lancashire Fusiliers); Douglas Fisher (Cameron Highlanders); Tony Southall (Caribineers); Anthony Bourne (Oxfordshire and Buckinghamshire Lt. Inf.); Tony Chambers (Lothian and Border Horse); Douglas Keith (51st. Div. Signals); Joe Carry (51st. Div. Signals).

(Front Row)—Roger Stewart (51st. Div. R.A.S.C.); Plug Harrington (Lancashire Fusiliers); E. M. Viney (Oxfordshire and Buckinghamshire Lt. Inf.); Ewart Gameson (Argyll and Sutherland Highlanders); Sandy Jenkins (Argyll and Sutherland).

It was possible to discuss religion with almost anyone, including some who before the war wouldn't even have allowed such a conversation to begin. It soon became clear that there existed within the camp a wide range of beliefs, together with non-adherence to any faith. The self-proclaimed atheists or agnostics were just as interesting to talk to as the believers, if only to discover their reasons.

Spasmodic but nevertheless prolonged study over many months revealed answers to the simpler questions, leading me eventually to having a word with the Roman Catholic chaplain. He was a weedy looking priest who had been caught in Crete and whose battle-dress seemed wholly out of place on him, but, as I came to learn later, a man of great courage with an outstanding intellect. After some months of talking to him on and off, I began to learn something about the Catholic Church, but there was still a great deal I didn't understand. Far from being swept forward in some new religious fervour, I was discouraged from continuing the discussions and advised to drop the whole thing and to continue attending the Church of England services.

With hindsight it was probably unwise of me to have mentioned this curiosity about other religions in a letter home. Sadly, it upset my mother though at the time I didn't really know why. Mainly as a result of a letter from my mother I tried to put all further thoughts about Roman Catholicism out of my mind.

Passing the days

What did we do all day? Much the same, I suppose, as in all the camps we were ever in. Much of our time was taken up with daily exercising, keeping our clothes and ourselves clean, reading and, for me, working in the library. We formed ourselves into small groups of six or so and shared between us the various tasks involved in preparing whatever we happened to have in the way of supplementary food. Many of us were indebted to one officer, probably a Royal Engineer, who had long since designed a means of cooking by the clever conversion of two of the larger tins, which were occasionally found in Red Cross parcels. These tins were fixed one on top of the other, and the base of the lower one was somehow raised a few inches; then, by creating a hole low down at the side for fuel intake and to provide a means for air to be drawn in, it became possible to produce a flame. This flame had to be fed continuously with balls of rolled up paper and unaccountably to me; there was virtually no smoke. It was certainly adequate to use as a mini-cooker and in a very short while endless examples of this new invention could be seen all over the camp.

Towards the end of the year some of the Red Cross parcels, which had at last started to arrive once more, contained small Christmas puddings. There sometimes would also be a small packet of egg powder, which could be made into custard. I attempted to do this on Christmas Day, but failed to heed the warning that if heated too long it would become scrambled egg. It did. But even scrambled egg on Christmas pudding though somewhat bizarre was a luxury not to be missed.

One of the most interesting occupations involved being one of a small number to whom the BBC news was read every evening. There was already more

Stove made from milk cans, from "Joe in Germany"

1943

OFLAG VII·B.

BEST WISHES FOR CHRISTMAS AND THE NEW YEAR.

Christmas cards with a touch of nostalgia. In the clouds, Oflag VIIb camp.

than one radio in the camp, and because it was assumed that the Germans were aware of this, the sets – still dismantled and reassembled every day – had to be protected by our own very thorough security measures, which included several readings of the news around the camp. We would assemble at a given time with 'lookouts' in position and take down, as quickly as each could manage in his own brand of shorthand, everything we were told on a very small piece of paper. We were given strict instructions that if on our way back to our respective Blocks we were confronted by a guard we were to swallow the incriminating piece of paper, which is why we always had it ready in hand to stuff in our mouths at a moment's notice. The only person ever to actually have to do this was myself; and on one occasion I had to do it very hurriedly indeed. That night I had to relay the news to my own and two other Blocks entirely from memory.

Sometimes rather more subtle methods were used to discover information about our radio. The German 'Sergeant-Major' who worked with us from time to time in the Technical Library, and who was reasonably friendly, broke the news to me one morning that Tobruk had fallen. I was just about to reply, "Yes, I know" when I recalled how I had come to hear of it, and so quickly appeared dutifully surprised.

From time to time there would be air-raid warnings and it would be heartening to see squadrons of American 'Flying Fortresses' on their bombing missions to targets not so very far from where we were. Eichstaat was fairly safe, mainly because it was known we were there, but on these occasions we all had to stay inside. The Germans would become very jittery during these raids and it was imperative to get inside very quickly. One officer, who didn't, was shot; and another who left cover to go to his help was shot as well. The death of these two caused deep concern to us all. On the next parade, and indeed for several days afterwards, we maintained absolute silence. It was remarkable how effective utter silence could be. The Germans went about their counting as usual but clearly they were ill-at-ease and nervous not knowing quite what to expect.

The Hitler Youth Movement

Occasionally we would see youths of sixteen or so in their brown Nazi uniforms being marched along the road outside. A 'friendly' guard told me that these members of the Hitler Jugend were moulded into the Nazi way of life from the age of ten, sometimes even earlier. The youths, he said, had to undergo rigorous training and every year had to pass an oral examination on the history of Germany since the First World War. Apparently one of the catch questions was: "And what comes after the Third Reich?" – that being the Government of the day. One wretched boy was almost certain to answer: "The Fourth Reich." "Dumkopf!" would come the reply, "Nothing comes after the Third Reich, because the Third Reich will go on for ever!" My informant didn't seem to think that there was anything wrong with teaching youths of such tender years how to hate; to kill, or maim others. Nor how appalling it was that these teenagers should be taught to accept that such violence was praiseworthy and an essential part of their patriotic duty to their fatherland. One of the fruits of such teaching came to light during the Normandy landings a year later, when the Hitler Jugend subsequently massacred fifty Canadian prisoners-of-war.

More escapes…

It took just over three years but eventually agreement was reached for the repatriation of those few prisoners who had been severely wounded or whose health was giving cause for serious concern. The exchange took place in 1943 and we said farewell to those who were going home and who were loaded with messages for many of our families. The knowledge that this exchange was going to happen at all was sufficient incentive to one officer to seek what he hoped would be an easy way out. He feigned some sort of insanity for several weeks, even deceiving some of his fellow officers; but it turned out to be a highly dangerous tactic, which, although resulting in his return to England, ended in him becoming genuinely and permanently insane.

The return of those repatriated in this way provided the War Office with their first information about a number of events that occurred in France in 1940, including the massacre at Wormhout.

For those of us left in Oflag VIIb, the most popular alternative way home was still by digging. The incentive to escape and to sense once again that long lost taste of freedom led many to lead the life of a mole. In fact by this time most of us could have been classified in one of four categories.

The first category included those who were almost fanatical in the desire to escape and who devoted each and every day to searching out means of doing so. These were mainly, but by no means wholly, professional officers to whom the effect of imprisonment was likely to have the most grievous impact. It deprived them of the opportunity to distinguish themselves and of the rapid promotion that so often takes place in war-time. Hence the persistent urge to salve what they could of their careers by at least making efforts to escape.

Glosters' at Oflag VII b.

The second, and much larger, category consisted of those who certainly wanted to escape but who tended to wait for others to initiate ideas about how to do so in the vague hope that they might be invited to join in some specific attempt.

The vast majority, however, were in the third category. These had long since decided that only a very limited number were going to be able to escape anyway, and so had abandoned any prospect of doing so themselves. They were the ones who consequently tried to make the best of their surroundings by taking what opportunities there were for study, or by using whatever artistic or other talents they possessed for their own benefit as well as others. They, and the previous category, were certainly very willing to help others in their attempts to escape.

The very few in the fourth category comprised those who were totally hostile to escaping. Whilst not deliberately obstructive they could nevertheless be something of a risk in their casual attitude to security. It was largely because of this that internal security had to be strictly maintained, with the result that hardly anyone was aware of the escape plans of others. On one occasion two tunnels converged on each other without either of those involved having any idea what the others were up to.

The Germans were well aware that tunnelling was a major pastime. They expected them and took all sorts of countermeasures. At Eichstaat this even included secreting an English-speaking soldier into the roof space above one of the huts whilst we were all on parade. The wretched spy cannot have learnt anything very much from any conversations he may have heard in the room below because, all too soon for him, he gave himself away by some noise and was soon discovered and hounded out. Other such measures included echo-sounding devices, which could somehow detect any hollow places; and the almost daily examination of earth around the camp.

In order to avoid collapse, tunnels had to be strengthened by any kind of wooden slat such as those that supported the palliasses on which we slept. After as many of these had been collected as was possible, plus a few extra supports from various other sources, there still remained many other problems. Movement within the tunnels was so restricted that unless a sort of chamber was incorporated it was not possible to turn round to get back out; and coming out backwards was a slow and painful process especially on the elbows. Snap parades could be called at any time, and anyone who happened to be in the middle – or worse, at the end – of a tunnel would be hard pressed to turn up either reasonably clean or on time.

It seemed curious that with the acute discomfort and its many hazards, tunnelling was the most favoured method of escape. Even a sixty-meter tunnel would take months of laborious work to complete, with the ever-present risk of discovery becoming more likely as the task progressed. With insufficient oxygen to keep a match alight, it became essential – more especially for the diggers – to find a way of circulating the damp air in the utter darkness within. As no give-away shaft could be pushed up to the surface, makeshift bellows had to be made and would be operated continuously in an effort to fan the air so that from time to time a match or candle could be used to illuminate what always seemed to me little more than a prison within prison. Yet most of those who succeeded in escaping, even for an hour, did so by choosing this painstaking, gruelling and claustrophobic route.

Improving the mind

The majority, who were not involved in any such schemes, had already turned their minds to how best to improve themselves by embarking on a particular course of study, or by developing their talents for art, writing, music or drama. It took a great deal of determination and perseverance to pursue any of these subjects at all seriously because of the constant interruptions, lack of privacy and the overall abiding, simple, yet pressing, daily needs of ensuring one's own survival in body and mind.

I found the time to study Spanish for a while, and even took The Royal Society of Arts written examination in the subject whilst still in the camp. In addition, I was one of several who gave a series of lessons to some of our orderlies, who were anxious to advance their own education. There were three in my 'class', and I did my best to instruct them in English grammar and composition. One of my friends whose subject was geography found it heavy going because most maps were forbidden and his two pupils seemed to be unusually lacking in any knowledge of the world. One morning he greeted them with the question: "Do either of you know what the Baltic is?" One of them replied: "Well, it's a parasite, innit?" I thought I was having my leg pulled but my friend swore it was true.

All this time military discipline, though much more relaxed, was never lost. It was certainly implemented by a self-imposed personal discipline, which was of paramount importance. Very few were ever observed to be letting themselves go, and those who showed signs of weakening in this way were mostly helped to return to at least some form of self-respect.

During these years the various temptations on offer in normal life were, as one friend put it, distressingly few. Consequently, there was little choice but to pursue a reasonably innocent life free from wine and women, but we did have a song; not that there was much to sing about for some time to come. At one stage quite early on, someone had had the bright idea of organising a "Song Contest." Each contestant, and there was no shortage of entries, had to sing a set piece called "Dinah," to be followed by a second song of their own choice. Some of the most unexpected officers entered the contest and preformed to the huge enjoyment of us all in the audience, who had the task of indicating by our applause the singers who we thought were the best. Some of our enthusiasm must have been very misleading as we displayed special warmth to one or two officers whose voices were nothing to write home about but whose boldness in appearing at all, coupled maybe with some personal mannerisms, brought forth the loudest cheers. The contest proved highly successful as it revealed a number of very good voices amongst us, several of whom went on later to entertain us at either concerts or in theatrical performances.

There were also a few talented actors with us, who with some help from amateurs, managed to put on several plays. Their task was made all the harder by all female roles having to be played by men. In addition there were all sorts of restrictions about costumes, which the Germans feared might be used by would-be escapees. These handicaps taxed the producers' resourcefulness to the utmost, nevertheless some of the plays were very good indeed, and had some no less remarkable scenery.

'Hooch'

The lack of alcohol was overcome by a few who discovered a method of making it. They somehow acquired a melon, or rather several, and as such fruit was never seen by the rest of us, we could only assume that a guard susceptible to bribery – as a few were – had been responsible for their sudden appearance. The top of the melon would be cut off and the seeds removed. The vacant space would then be filled with sugar or syrup plus one or two other ingredients and the top securely replaced. It was then left for several weeks hanging outside, if possible, during which time fermentation would take place producing a sort of crude melon wine. When distilled by boiling and cooling the steam, a disappointing amount of alcohol could be obtained. This would be saved up and added to repeated efforts with more melons until such time as a sufficient quantity had been accumulated to a warrant 'party.' The alcohol was of fairly high strength and its effect upon those brave or foolhardy enough to drink it was startling.

One Christmas evening several normally respectable officers, only too clearly affected by this new spirit, were seen celebrating in a manner more usually associated with an annual Rugby Club dinner. I was trying to make myself heard in an effort to read out the news that evening, in the same room, and by a curious coincidence, found myself saying: "In his Christmas broadcast this afternoon, King George VI referred to the dignified way in which British prisoners-of-war were conducting themselves in the hands of the enemy." At that very moment at least three officers were swinging wildly like monkeys from the top of one three-tier bed to another, emitting raucous animal noises as they did so.

A second reprisal

Earlier that autumn came the second major act of retaliation or reprisal. One morning assembling for a routine parade, it was noticed that the perimeter sentry boxes had their flaps down and that machine guns were at the ready, being aimed straight at us. The last few to turn up in each section were ordered well away from the rest and made to form a group of their own at the other end of the parade ground. The Kommandant then addressed us on roughly the following lines: "It has come to the notice of the High Command that some German prisoners-of-war taken by the British in North Africa have been handcuffed, or had their hands chained together, in contravention of the terms of the Geneva Convention. Orders have therefore been given for the same number of British prisoners-of-war to be similarly chained. This order will be put into effect at once."

Quite clearly the Kommandant expected this announcement to lead to an immediate riot, hence the military preparedness. In addition, as became clear much later, he had a white handkerchief in his hand, which, if dropped, would have been the signal for the machine guns to open fire. Mortars were even strategically sited in the hills around the camp, poised to fire their shells on us if the rioting became too much for his men to control. But there was no riot.

The general reaction was one of bemusement, and a keen desire to see which of our friends were in the late arrival squad, who were about to have their hands chained together. A contingent of armed guards quickly arrived on the scene carrying dozens of dangling chains; and all those destined for this treatment were duly chained and led off to a block where they were to be together for the next month or so. The chains were removed at night and brought back in the morning, when they were reapplied. Some of the guards whose duty it was to do this were clearly not at all that happy with their orders, and on the whole it appeared that many of them found the operation as degrading to themselves as it was to those who were chained. As with all the reprisals, this was a political decision and did not stem from the German High Command.

During visits to those now known as the 'Chain Gang,' some of the more restricting aspects of the chaining became apparent. For instance, it was not possible to put your hands behind your back, which could at certain times have very inconvenient disadvantages. Not that it mattered for long because on the day following the initial chaining it was discovered how to unlock them. It proved to be remarkably simple and could be done using a sardine-tin opener. The guards soon became aware of this and some of them would come into the rooms and leave the chains there asking the gang to put them on themselves, warning them not to be caught without them on. Rather like the first reprisal, this one petered out after a while and then suddenly stopped without any explanation.

The Gestapo

Some weeks later the whole camp was subject to a major search, and for the first time this included a number of plain-clothed men from the Gestapo. It was the first time that we were to see the military adopt the Nazi salute, which had recently become compulsory for all the armed forces. The universal army salute was now replaced by the raised right arm accompanied by the words: "Heil Hitler!" The search took the whole of one day, and we were kept outside whilst every possession was examined in detail and every inch of our rooms searched with the usual thoroughness. We were also individually searched. Any books, letters and even small pieces of paper that did not bear a German censor's stamp were removed for further detailed scrutiny.

Being somewhat bored with the whole procedure, one enterprising officer livened things up by seizing an opportunity to remove a pistol, loaded as it happened, from an inattentive Gestapo officer. When the search was finally concluded, an appeal had to be made over the loud speakers for the pistol's return. "You British officers have had your bit of fun, but now you must return this pistol." Nothing happened, and after some delay a second appeal was made but this time accompanied by dire threats about what would happen if the pistol was not returned at once. The officer responsible, who claimed to be hard of hearing and so had not heard nor understood the announcements, came forward and gave it up saying that he had found the pistol "lying around," and was going to hand it in as lost property at the end of the day anyway, so what was all the fuss about? The Gestapo officer stepped forward to receive it with obvious embarrassment and to the barely concealed amusement of the Kommandant, his staff and, indeed, all of us. But this was not all. Another of our number had noticed earlier on this very warm day that a Gestapo Officer had removed his cap and leather jacket. Scooping up these two items he managed, presumably unseen, to secrete them in a rubbish dump. The eventual demand for their return was similar to that for the pistol. The cap and the jacket had to be returned but were by then covered in dirt and grime. On being allowed to return to our rooms, we checked through our belongings to see if anything was missing and most recorded some item or other - usually food, though rarely cigarettes.

The cigarette was still the only accepted unit of currency and its importance became even more apparent when three imaginative officers set up a 'shop' within the camp. These three priced a whole range of items, from a variety of foods to all sorts of personal belongings, in relation to a certain number of cigarettes. All the cigarettes came from Britain in limited supplies and non-smokers had an equal chance with smokers to acquire this 'currency.' Money remained virtually meaningless - the prisoner-of-war paper money being largely regarded as useless.

A convert to Catholicism

This year of 1943 became a memorable one for me because in the midst of it I found myself concerned once again with probing into the mysteries – as they appeared to me then – of the Roman Catholic faith. I sought further talks with the Catholic chaplain, who didn't appear at all surprised that I should want to see him again. At all sorts of times and in the very few places where it was possible to hold a private conversation, we discussed every aspect of the Catholic faith. All my questions were patiently answered, and in the autumn I started on a course of instruction.

I had all along been very conscious of my mother's plea not to come to any hasty conclusion about my religious faith, and her urging me to defer any final decision until I returned home. She also vaguely hinted that my state of mind after three and a half years as a prisoner-of-war might not be balanced enough to enable me to think clearly and dispassionately about so important a matter; and, anyway, a prison camp was no place in which to make such a decision. I understood her feelings and anxiety for me and thought about it all for quite a long time.

I eventually concluded that my mind was in quite good order, and that there was at least one advantage of studying this matter where I was. The mere fact of just being there made it possible to think about it all for as long as was necessary; and in a detached way free from any emotional ties or influences from family or close friends – no pressures of any kind and least of all from the chaplain himself. He, unlike a busy parish priest, had as much time on his hands as I had, and was therefore able to give me all the time I needed.

Questions, arguments and discussions all played their part, but they were not the only factors that lead to me convert from the Anglican, or Protestant faith to Roman Catholicism. Several other converts to whom I have spoken since have expressed a similar view. I cannot recall exactly when, nor indeed how, I came to a final realisation that the Catholic Church possessed the whole truth and, most importantly, the authority to teach it. All I can recall is that at some stage or other I ceased to have any doubts at all, and consequently was eager to make the change as soon as possible. The thought of waiting until the end of the war had no appeal. There was anyway no certainty that we would ever get back home, and as will be made clear later, some of us indeed didn't do so. It would be understandable for anyone who has not shared such an experience to fail to appreciate that having found a treasure – the anxiety to possess it completely and without delay is overwhelming.

On Christmas Eve, 1943, at a little ceremony with only one friend present, I was formally received into the Catholic Church by the chaplain, and so attended his Christmas Mass the following day.

It would be another fifteen years before I came to learn of the strong Catholic background of my forefathers; or of them being listed amongst some of the well known recusant families of the sixteenth century. Amongst these was an ancestor Blessed Thomas Belson, a young layman, who was incarcerated in the Tower of London on two occasions and later hanged in Oxford, in 1589, at the age of twenty-six, for his unwavering adherence to his faith. Two priests whom he had helped, and a servant, were hanged with him. Thomas was one of eighty-five martyrs to be beatified by Pope John Paul II in November 1987.

Converts, as I have come to learn, tend to make themselves unbearable by their obvious happiness and resulting over-enthusiastic attitude to life generally. They are anxious to share what they have found, only to realise all too quickly that others are not particularly interested and anyway are probably hoping they will shut up about it. It is rather like being a bit merry after a drink or two and suddenly finding yourself in somewhat sober company.

I can only hope I avoided any excessive exuberance, but as I write this almost sixty years later, I cannot forget the elation I experienced at the time; and although this joy has been tempered by so many years it is still very much with me today. It is one of the only two major decisions in my life about which I have never had any doubts nor any regrets.

In the few letters we were allowed to write, I tried to explain to my parents and two brothers what I had done and why. The men in my family appeared not to be all that interested and seemed to shrug off the news as one of those things that could easily happen to anyone locked away for so long, and "anyway, it could have been worse!" My mother, on the other hand, expressed her concern but accepted the situation though it must have caused her some pain, which I hadn't found any way of avoiding.

Meanwhile I came to know much better other Catholics in the camp, two of whom later became Godfathers to our eldest and youngest children. Luckily, the Kommandant, who was Catholic himself, ensured that there was a Chapel as well as everything that was needed for it. He may have seen to this on his own initiative, or possibly have been influenced by the presence of the Papal Nuncio to Germany, who spent much of the war in Eichstaat, though we didn't know this at the time.

Whilst conversions to Catholicism went mainly unremarked, a conversion to Christian Science caused quite a ripple of interest. There was only one such case that I ever knew about and it was certainly an intriguing one. It so happened that the day following his conversion, the officer concerned was hit on the inside of his knee by a hard ball whilst playing a form of cricket. This unfortunate stroke of fate resulted in him being in obvious pain to the extent that he could hardly walk. He shunned all offers of help, maintaining stoically that there was nothing wrong at all, even refusing the offer of treatment in the Infirmary.

This incident taught me the essential difference between admiring, which I certainly couldn't fail to do, the sincerity of someone else's belief without necessarily admiring the belief itself.

The world beyond the camp…

For those whose captivity dated from Dunkirk, June 1943 marked the end on three years in Germany. There still seemed to be no end in sight to the war, despite some items of good news on our radio. The war was certainly not going to end in 1943, and it became increasingly obvious that an army would, at some time or other, have to land in France, for regardless of whatever could be achieved at sea or in the air, historically wars are won by infantry occupying enemy territory.

The first indication that this might happen at all came on September 3rd, the fourth anniversary of Britain's declaration of war with Germany. British and Canadian troops landed at *Reggio di Calabria*, and thus began the Allies' invasion of Italy. One day in the middle of the month there were enormous headlines in the German papers announcing "The Treachery of Italy", their ally, who had entered into and had now exited from the war within the time so many of us had been in Germany. On October 15th the Government of Italy declared war on Germany; not a very frightening prospect for the Germans but one which gave them a second front to worry about in Europe, at a time when they were suffering severe reverses on their eastern front.

All this news was highly encouraging and it seemed that the tide of war had truly turned. Inside Germany, however, the unrelenting slaughter of Jews continued on an even larger scale – news that we could not learn about at the time. Also included were thousands of Russian prisoners-of-war, partisans, dissidents, gypsies and the disabled in body or mind – a monumental brutal carnage unparalleled in history.

The spring of 1944 marked a most welcome turning point in our lives. The war news became much more encouraging and at last real hopes were kindled that we might see the end of it all that year. We could only guess at the enormous build-up and preparation in Britain for what we assumed would be an Anglo-American invasion across the Channel to somewhere in France. Meanwhile we had begun to learn about Hitler's new weapon. This was the V-1 missile, shortly followed by the V-2, which were being targeted at London.

Letters from home rarely mentioned such things, but it was certainly possible without having to read too closely between the lines to realise that life in England was becoming increasingly harsh. It was clear that much damage had been done by these new weapons, which were fired indiscriminately and could land anywhere. Many homes had been destroyed and families rendered homeless. One memorable letter informed a fellow prisoner that his elderly father had had a narrow escape in an air raid, which had demolished his house. The old man had been picked up out of the rubble unconscious but, amazingly, barely scratched. When eventually asked what he could remember of the incident, he was reported to have replied; "I remember being in the upstairs loo and when I pulled the chain the house fell down!"

Another letter came from a presumably conscious-stricken wife who asked the husband she hadn't seen for three years if he thought it a good idea for her to adopt a baby. The officer concerned replied that he wasn't too worried and left the decision to her. It eventually transpired that his wife had gone to a maternity home three months later and had given birth to twins.

Amidst all these troubles, life changed dramatically for the better on the 7th June, the day after the landings in France. The German papers announced in huge headlines 'Anglo-American Invasion under Soviet direction'. As Russia had nothing to do with the direction of this invasion, we could only assume that the mention of the Soviets was an attempt to diffuse the importance of the initiative, which was in fact wholly Anglo-American. This, we thought, was it. Everyone became far more cheerful for we all knew that now at last British and American troops had set foot on the same territory from which we had been driven four years before.

We felt sure that we should be home for Christmas; but some, so full of confidence to begin with, found their hopes fading in the face of all sorts misgivings. It was a time to think more realistically about what life might mean for us when we did get back. How would we feel amongst our old friends? Would we be embarrassed in the company of those who had fought a war, many considerably younger than ourselves? What would they have to say to us? What could we talk about? Who would want to hear about the sort of life we had been leading? Such questions were impossible to answer but they left many of us with an uneasy feeling that getting home again, thoughts of which had dominated our years of captivity, might just possibly turn out to be something of an anti-climax.

Meanwhile, the Germans were ever anxious to discover what might really be going on in the camp right under their noses. What current schemes were under way for escaping? Where was the radio hidden, and how had it survived searches? Were forbidden materials finding their way into the camp, and if so, how? Were any of their own guards succumbing to bribery?

Phoney prisoners-of war

One of the more desperate ruses employed to seek out answers to such questions was to infiltrate a phoney prisoner-of-war to live amongst us, and in such way that would fail to arouse the hint of any suspicion. To have any chance of success the 'stooge' would have to be very well trained, speak perfect English and work quickly. Living voluntarily as a prisoner-of-war with us would give him every incentive to seek out the information required with the minimum of delay; yet in acting too hastily he would very soon risk being uncovered. Our own security arrangements were such that newcomers unknown to any of us, and especially those who arrived alone, were closely questioned in an effort to establish their true identity.

One such person, a Belgian officer, was brought into the camp on his own in the summer of 1944 and aroused immediate suspicion. Under questioning, he claimed that he had been serving as an interpreter with the U.S. Army and had been captured in a German counter-offensive in the Ardennes, an attack that had taken place earlier in the year and about which we were already aware. When asked if he could identify himself by naming anyone in the British Army with whom it might be possible to check his story, he replied that he only knew of one British officer and he was a prisoner-of-war named Philip Varley. Philip, whom I hardly knew at the time though have come to know well since, was summoned to confront the newcomer but affirmed at once that he had never met him before.

In the ensuing conversation that took place, however, it became clear that the Belgian had been billeted with Philip's parents in England and consequently knew his family, his house, which he could describe, and that their son was a prisoner-of-war somewhere in Germany. He could hardly have expected to meet him personally in the same camp, nor that such meeting would give him the perfect opportunity to prove his identity.

A sequel to this episode occurred in April 1945 in the debacle described later, just two weeks before the end of the war as we were leaving Eichstaat for our final camp. In the confusion at the time the Belgian, who was multi-lingual and may have been involved in Intelligence operations, managed to slip away and was back in England within a few days. He was thus able to telephone Philip's parent, telling them that he had seen their son; that all was well with him and that there was very hope that they would see him home again very soon.

Preparing for the return home

Any further thoughts of being home for Christmas 1944 were dashed as by September it had become obvious that we were destined to spend another winter in Germany. Unlike other winters, though, this one was lightened by the widely held conviction that it would be the last. By means of our invaluable radio, we were able each day to follow the progress of the war on both western and eastern fronts; and early in 1945 the news was even more encouraging. In February we received first hand information about how things were at home from an RAF pilot, who was shot down and who ended up in our camp. I don't doubt that many of us had become very introspective and the advent of this officer gave us a welcome insight into what was going on in the rest of the world – a world in which we should now start taking a deeper interest. His view on the war was highly encouraging, and he reckoned that it was only a matter of months, maybe even weeks, before the German capitulation. His view about us, however, was far from comforting. To begin with he couldn't believe that a number of us had already actually been in Germany for over four years. One of my friends was rash enough to ask him if he thought we were mentally in good order, to which he responded with the chilling reply: "Frankly, no!" We never asked any newcomer the same question again.

One evening in March, we heard on our radio a psychologist give a rather disturbing talk on how relatives should treat returning prisoners-of-war. We were not to be asked any questions; no reference was to be made to our captivity; we were to be expected to behave from time to time in a rather irrational way, and no notice must be taken of this. Relatives were also warned that we might have developed all sorts of unconventional habits. The talk went on and on and became for us, who probably weren't expected to be able to listen to it, more and more depressing.

Having now had years in which to reflect upon this advice, I think it was certainly well intentioned, but the fact that we did actually hear it only added to our apprehension about meeting relatives again, knowing that they were likely to observe what they had been advised. Thus, the potential was created for an additional strain to be put on relationships already suffering from the effects of such long absence. For many, as I came to learn, it also had a rather sad effect. There is something wholly abnormal about going through any major experience in life, good or bad, and yet not to talk about it even to close family or friends; but only conversing with those who happened to have shared the same experience. The situation is akin to that of an active man suddenly struck dumb as a result of a stroke; yet abnormal as it may seem it was by no means unusual.

The war was clearly coming to an end. All sorts of rumours were rife in the camp, the least attractive of which was that before capitulating Hitler had given orders that all prisoners-of-war should be shot. This rumour was not taken lightly and, to counteract this possibility, measures were actually drawn up to deal with such an emergency; though what they were I never found out.

Air attack

At the beginning of April, 1945, we were given orders for our final move: this time to Moosberg, a place used at the end of the First World War as a collecting point for prisoners-of-war of all nationalities. On the morning of Palm Sunday, whilst we were preparing ourselves for the early morning departure, we saw across the valley an American fighter plane swoop down, and blow up a lorry moving along the road before returning in the direction whence it came.

The Senior British Officer gave orders that as we were approaching the end of the war, we were to march properly and not straggle along as had become our practice until then. We were formed up into groups of a hundred, the first few groups to leave the camp waited along a straight road adjoining the camp perimeter, whilst the other groups formed up behind. When all was eventually ready we marched off accompanied by a number of guards, some of whom were showing signs of losing all interest in what they were doing. We had hardly started before we saw the sudden return of the American fighter plane, which to our horror flew straight at us blazing away with both its machine guns. There was no cover to be found anywhere and, although we scattered as best we could, there was no way of hiding from the plane, nor from the second one that appeared. By this time the first one had circled round and was just starting another sweep right along the road, firing directly into the whole column. Quite a number were killed outright including several Germans. Many others were severely wounded; a friend lay near me, face down, with one leg completely split open though he was still fully conscious. I recognised a fellow Catholic, who had been hit in the chest. Catching sight of the chaplain, who was darting around amongst the wounded, I was able to direct him to my friend just moments before he died.

This was one of the most unexpected and frightening attacks I had ever experienced, and it drove several of our group to attempt to climb back over the perimeter wire and back into the camp we had just left. Luckily for us that was the end of the attack, and we were all ordered back to the camp. The pilot of the first plane was shot down soon afterwards, and we were to meet him later at Moosberg. It appeared that he had mistaken us for German troops because, as he explained: "Prisoners-of-war do not march, they straggle." In addition, some 50 German army packs neatly stacked in rows, each topped with a German helmet gave the impression in the sunlight glinting off them that it was a tank. He was deeply cut up about what he had done, but not so much as we were. It was particularly sad to lose a friend after so long a time in captivity, but even worse to what is ludicrously called 'friendly fire.'

After several more chaotic days at the camp we had never expected to return to so suddenly, we left once again – pointedly straggling this time – at night, under cover of darkness. Apparently infrared light already in use at that stage of the war could easily have spotted us, but thankfully we were unaware of this hazard. It took a week to reach our destination. We rested during the day and trudged on in the dark.

Our guards were already showing a marked change in attitude as they clearly saw that the war for them was almost over. One of them asked me if I would sign a chit saying that he was an Austrian and a 'good fellow', not really a German at all and certainly not a Nazi. I declined, but learnt later that he had succeeded in obtaining a chit from someone else, though what was written on it he wouldn't have known because his English was very limited. One aged guard alongside me during one of these night treks was obviously in distress and was having difficulty in keeping up. I offered to carry his light machine gun for him, and did so for long enough to render it useless by ramming paper and anything else to hand up the barrel. I had a sudden thought – what was I doing? This was the first time in the war that I had had a gun, and a machine gun at that, and there I was making it unserviceable!

Moosberg

Moosberg was a vast collection camp, divided into several compounds to cater for Americans, Russians and other nationalities as well as ourselves. During the two weeks we were there the number of guards decreased, so there was no need to conceal our radio which was at its most useful just then. On 25th April, we learnt that the Americans were only some forty miles away. At noon on 28th April, an American tank broke down the main gate and stormed into the camp to stupendous cheering. The Kommandant, who had remained, surrendered himself and all the remaining guards to an American General.

So ended just under five years as a prisoner-of-war.

FREE AT LAST

But although freed, we had to stay where we were for another week. It was the longest week I can remember ever having spent anywhere. To add to our dismay; we were kept in at gunpoint by our American allies while we tried to come to terms with a 'liberation', that meant no freedom as yet, no bread, no potatoes, nothing to celebrate with, not even any fuel for the stoves - and to cap it all, it was snowing.

This last week was one of utter chaos. Many Russians soon broke loose from their compound and were quickly involved in an orgy of drunkenness, rape and murder. Maybe they knew, or at least suspected, that if they ever returned to Russia they would probably be shot – as indeed many were. At last, arrangements were made for us to be taken by the truckload to an air landing strip in the middle of nowhere to be flown to France whence we would eventually be flown to England. The first day we sat around from early morning to dusk, to no avail. Some did leave in a few Dakotas, but space was very limited, most of us had to return for another night in camp.

We were back again the following morning, and whilst waiting around on the grass a 'plane circled right overhead. Looking more closely we could see that it had German markings. No one seemed to be in the least concerned, even when it landed on some rough ground nearby. Two German pilot officers jumped out, clicked their heels, saluted and surrendered themselves and their 'plane to us. No one seemed to know what to do with them; though their 'plane might have come in handy just then if only someone had known how to fly it. Few of us had ever been *in* an aircraft much less flown one. The two pilots looked highly relieved that we were British rather than Russian or even American. Nothing much happened until one of us shouted: "Oh! Do go away!" They got the message, saluted again and, abandoning their plane, left to try their luck somewhere else.

At last one of the Dakota aircraft gave me my first flight ever, and we landed somewhere in France, but I have no recollection of where. It didn't seem to matter, as we were only there a short while. Just before embarking on a Lancaster Bomber, which was to bring us back to England, someone, gave me an orange, a fruit I hadn't seen for years. I ate it greedily and it was wonderful. The interior of the plane was primitive in the extreme: hardly any seating, loose cables all over the place, and we had to squat down wherever we could, but what did that matter either? - we were about to come home. We had complete confidence in our RAF pilot, even though he looked young enough to have only left school the previous week.

Tragically, as we were to hear later, one plane crashed on the way back because a nerve-wracked officer clutched at a loose cable, which happened to activate the rudder, thus causing the pilot to lose control of the aircraft. Another plane crashed into electricity cables during its descent on to English soil, and all were killed. There could hardly have been more devastating accidents to happen to those who, having spent so long in Germany, were then on their very last lap home.

We were lucky as our young pilot landed us safely at an airfield in Buckinghamshire. But for me all was not well. The orange I had eaten so hurriedly at the airfield in France had an appalling effect on my inside and I was doubled up with acute stomach gripes. On disembarking I was whisked away to see a doctor, and was immediately packed off to Amersham Hospital, where I was told I had eaten too much pith. This was not quite the wonderful homecoming I had been looking forward to for so long, especially as I was kept there for three days. During this time my mother had been informed where I was, but in the excitement of the moment she couldn't remember whether the Hospital was in Amesbury, Aylesbury or Amersham, and her informant hadn't left a telephone number. She found me eventually, and we were reunited in a ward, where I was given the all clear and taken home.

PART SIX

Coming Home

"For there is nothing either good or bad,
but thinking makes it so"

Hamlet, II, ii

HOMECOMING was the occasion of very mixed feelings: heartfelt relief for having arrived back safely and to have found both parents well, though clearly affected by the weariness of war, and to have learnt that both brothers were also safe and sound; but real anxiety about problems to be faced in so many directions. For now, though, it was time to celebrate just being together again.

Enquiries about my contemporaries of 1939 brought little good news, or indeed any information at all. They seemed either to have been killed or to be serving in the Forces scattered around the world, probably in the Far East. A few of my older, much older, friends were still around, but I had no inkling of the difficulties involved in getting to see anyone who was beyond walking distance. Public transport was distinctly patchy, and even if we had had a car it wouldn't have been much use as petrol was very strictly rationed.

I did, however, come to see for myself during this long leave enough of the immense damage in central London caused by the indiscriminate bombing by the V-1 and V-2 missiles. Huge gaps in streets where houses or offices had stood brought home something of the anguish that the whole country had suffered, especially during the last two years. I was soon to meet a young woman who told me that, with her husband away on service overseas and her two young children evacuated to a supposedly safe haven in Cornwall, she had returned from work one evening to find her house completely destroyed by a bomb. Alone and suddenly homeless, her utter desolation only deepened as she realised that every possession, every material memory of her life, had been obliterated in an instant with no hope of recovery – and she was but one of hundreds who suffered in this way.

In that May of 1945, Britain was indeed in a desolate state. In addition to the enormous military and civilian casualties, over half a million houses had been destroyed and thousands more severely damaged. Everything, including schools, hospitals and social services, was woefully disrupted. The urgent need to start rebuilding was only too obvious, but the economic state of the country was such that it imposed a superhuman task on anyone with the courage even to consider attempting it.

To me, in this very new England, there was much evidence of the "Blood, toil, tears and sweat", which, in May 1940, Churchill had warned the country to expect; yet in the midst of so much material destruction, coupled with a deep piercing sorrow that had struck into the hearts of so many families, there was an unmistakable sense of relief. The fighting in Europe was over and it was now a time for recovery and renewed hope for all.

The elation at the defeat of the enemy, who had come so dangerously close to defeating us in our weakness of five years ago, was tempered to some extent by the enormous cost already paid in lives lost and by the incalculable price yet to be paid for victory. Much has been written about the indomitable spirit of the people of our nation – a spirit greatly enhanced by an underlying sense of humour, which helped to sustain so many in times of real trouble. It is curious that humour of any sort was hardly, if ever, apparent amongst the Germans we encountered and it certainly wouldn't appear to be characteristic of their nation. Even in wartime the ability to see some of the highly incongruous situations in which we found ourselves as laughable most assuredly lessened the tension and drama of the occasion. In this vastly changed England of 1945 we were going to need all the humour we could muster to cope with the aftermath of so long a war.

The major factor affecting every citizen in the country was the rationing of almost every necessity, particularly of food, and this was likely to continue for some years to come. Our, for the most part, law-abiding citizens had long since been conditioned to stand patiently in queues, to hand over their coupons to be cut out of their ration books and return home thankful to have received their fair share of whatever was available. Very rarely some unrationed food would suddenly appear on offer, and when it did the news spread so rapidly that lengthy queues would form within minutes, some optimists tagging along with no idea what they were queuing for, yet resolute that they were not going to miss an opportunity. One such person, I was told, eager to supplement her meagre meat ration, joined a queue only to find as she neared its head that 'Tales from Hoffman' was in fact a concert for which she was then expected to buy tickets. Amongst the less attractive non-rationed foods were squirrels, crows and, the least appealing of all, whale meat. The queues for this latter delicacy were rarely long as the pungent smell in the kitchen was more that enough to overwhelm the unfortunate cook.

The rationing of clothes affected women much more than men. Women, hard pressed to deck themselves out in any semblance of glamorous attire, had to resort to the very extremes of imaginative thinking in making the most out of what was available. The results of their efforts, using the few clothing coupons permitted, were often surprisingly graceful, elegant and, indeed, attractive. On the other hand, men, unburdened with the same impulse to ring the changes, could be seen bursting with patriotic pride, happily wearing their favourite, but dilapidated, old jackets and trousers, which in normal times would have long since been consigned by their wives to the dustbin or to some unsuspecting charity. It would be a long time before any sort of formal dress for either men or women would be taken out of mothballs. Austerity was destined to last for at least another five years.

As all alcoholic drinks were in exceedingly short supply, and as my pre-war involvement with wine had somehow conveniently been remembered, I found myself being pressed to use what influence I could muster to bring some cheer to relations and friends. During this long leave I went to Bristol to see my old firm, partly to seek reassurance that my job with them was still secure, which it was, and partly to sniff out any possibility of obtaining some much-needed supplies. The company was generous indeed and I came away far from empty handed. I also came to learn how severe the shortage was when a man came into the office during this visit and boldly asked for a dozen or more bottles of wines and spirits. He was most courteously told that the firm had nowhere near enough of anything to satisfy the wishes of even their existing long-standing accounts and so, regretfully, were as yet unable to take on any new ones. The man started to leave, but as he reached the door, turned and said, "Pity! You see I happen to run a goose farm in Somerset." The speed that an immediate deal was struck was breathtaking.

There were other, rather more sinister, ways of persuasion – such as that practised by my dentist. One day, lying back in his chair awaiting a filling, I saw him poised with a wicked looking drill, which he had already set in motion, and above its menacing grinding noise he chose that moment to ask: "Now, tell me, what's all this I hear about a shortage of whisky?" This brazen tactic reminded me of some of those who remained stubbornly silent under questioning in Germany, and who were then told "We hef ways of making you talk!"

With all these and endless other shortages it was hardly the best time to entertain or be entertained, yet within days it was time to celebrate VE Day – Victory in Europe. This brought forth invitations to parties, but I was markedly unenthusiastic about them. Yet parties and celebrations were just the sort of activities we had all been looking forward to for so long. What had gone wrong? It must be very difficult for anyone else to understand, especially so many years later. I just knew that within me there was this strange reluctance to meet people. It may have been anxiety about conversation; but it could have been the growing feeling of emptiness; a feeling of hardly belonging to their world at all.

In the mind

I doubt whether any of us returning from Germany ever gave a thought to the possible need for counselling, which doesn't mean that some, or maybe all, of us would not have benefited from it. The thought just didn't occur to us, as it had not occurred to us, as far as I know, during all those years, that the war might be lost; nor had we considered what might happen to us if indeed it *was* lost. It might be thought that for many who have been involved in some grim experience, whether in body or mind, the need for professional counselling may well be urgent, and that in most cases such treatment could successfully restore peace to a mind that had been severely shaken. Some experiences, however, whether wholly personal or witnessed in connection with others, can never be completely eradicated from the mind. They are the ones that have been written in indelible ink, and the greater the anxiety to expunge them from the memory the more deeply are they likely to be ingrained.

In our modern world, counselling has become an all too familiar option. In this new millennium, to suffer a minor accident, to lose someone dear, or to watch some horrifying television programme – even though it could be switched off at any time – can lead to a counsellor coming round to help you come to terms with your 'problem'. In 1945, although it may have been practised in some specific areas of treatment, counselling was not generally available, nor much thought of as any kind of necessity, which was probably just as well seeing that there could hardly have been anyone in Britain at that time who had escaped some traumatic experience.

By one of those curious coincidences in life, just as I began to write this narrative, some correspondence appeared in the press on this very subject. It seems that these letters were prompted by a prior reference to stress (not necessarily to do with prisoners-of-war) and how it was being dealt with in the services.

Whilst counselling for us may well have had its place, it just wasn't an option. By far the most appropriate treatment for most of us, though I hadn't heard of it at the time, would have been to follow the lead of the Father of Medicine, the Greek physician Hippocrates, born in the fifth century BC. He had had the foresight to establish his hospital on the Mediterranean island of Cos, where the sick were treated to a peaceful view, warm winds and the regenerating rhythm of waves breaking on the seashore – a place where a man could be healed because the natural order was allowed to reassert itself.

There wasn't much sign of any natural order in the England I had returned to, and an early feeling of unease hit me on the first Sunday at home. That morning I had set off on my own to walk to the local Catholic church, whilst my parents went to the Anglican church close by, which we all used to attend together before the war. Nothing much was said but the atmosphere somehow precluded easy conversation. I must have been a real problem son and regret so much having caused additional worry to my parents, who had had so much to put up with for so long and with constant anxiety about us, their three sons. To cap it all, their telephone number was only one digit different from that of the local Post Office. Throughout the war they received carelessly dialled calls from other Post Offices which always started with the words: "We have a telegram for you."

Sadly, that BBC talk that we had heard only some three months earlier, whilst still in Germany, with its advice about how relatives and friends should treat returning prisoners-of-war, was already having the very effect which had given rise to such foreboding amongst many of us at the time. It became abundantly clear very early on that anything to do with my experiences during the last five years was a taboo subject; and it was indeed studiously avoided by everyone I met, and even within the family. I felt at times rather akin to someone who had recently been bereaved. Those whom I met would, on occasion, talk with that awkwardness that can so easily arise when meeting such a person. It was only too easy to sense the restraint they were observing in their anxiety not to mention anything that might resurrect painful memories. Their thoughtfulness and consideration were genuinely appreciated but it didn't make for stimulating conversation, especially as I began to feel uncomfortable about making any reference to *their* war experiences. It thus became very clear – this conversational barrier worked both ways.

It was something of a relief to learn later that this situation did not in fact apply just to us in my own family, but also, in varying degrees, to many other families, and was by no means confined to returning prisoners-of-war. On the surface it may have appeared that an almost bizarre situation had arisen in which the momentous events of the last five years, events which had affected us all so dramatically wherever any of us may have been, were now virtually barred from conversation. The reason was not hard to determine. Most people by then were only too thankful to have survived the horrors of this appalling war, and for the time being anyway were in no mood to be reminded of it. War experiences were therefore somehow being consigned to a vast memory bank, to be drawn on later, much later, if ever.

Pondering on this one day, I concluded that it wasn't such a bad idea after all. Although psychologists talk about the latent hazards to even the physical well-being of those who bottle things up year after year, it seemed to me that the sooner it was all forgotten, the better. Maybe that radio speaker, whom we had found so worrying, had had more of a point than any of us in Germany could have imagined at the time. It is easy enough to want to forget, yet so much harder actually to do so; but this prevailing trend against reminiscences at least made it simpler.

After all the celebrations of VE Day in May 1945, it was time to remember that the war with Japan was yet to be won. I was still on active service but had begun to develop headaches that would last all day. These were no ordinary headaches; they were the severest I could remember; furthermore, they became increasingly worse. The doctor prescribed aspirins, but neither they nor anything else had any effect – the headaches just went on and on and on. No physical cause could be determined, so, it was concluded, the cause must be in the mind – not a very comforting revelation, and made even less so by the possibility of having to consult a psychiatrist. By one of life's curious coincidences, I was about to see one anyway.

One day when I happened to be in Piccadilly, I chanced upon a man I recognised at once as having been in the same camps as myself. I asked him what he was doing now and received the startling answer that he was now a trick cyclist. Not having heard this expression before, I enquired whether he performed on the stage or in a circus. "No, no!" he replied, "I'm now a fully qualified *psychiatrist.*" I persuaded him to join me in a nearby bar, where we began on some rather serious reflections on the years spent in captivity.

He explained that our years in Germany would assuredly have a whole range of both temporary and permanent effects. To begin with he was not very encouraging. Did I remember old so and so? Well, within a month of being back home all his hair fell out. And had I heard about another of our lot who had returned home to discover that his wife had been married to someone else for over two years; and how he had decided to kill himself; and how he was restrained at the very last minute from throwing himself off the Clifton Suspension Bridge? He began to speak of someone else we both knew and could probably have continued with several more as he was obviously intrigued by them. But I had heard enough, and it wasn't what I wanted to hear at all. He then asked me how I was, but suspecting that he might find some reason to scoop me up as an addition to his list of woe, I carefully avoided any mention of my depressing headaches. With my apparent good health and no alarming stories to relate about myself, his professional interest in me took a steep dive. He might have left if I hadn't persuaded him to linger a bit longer.

I was glad he stayed because he began to talk more seriously about the likely effects of long-term captivity, stressing two in particular. The most significant of these would be loss of self-esteem; not that anyone would try to make us feel small; rather, we would feel that we had been left behind in a world that, because of the war, had advanced so rapidly and in so many directions at the same time. He had observed this feeling in a number of others and reckoned that it would last for some time but should eventually wear off. This was a bit more encouraging, though he added that there might well be a few who would retain a sense of inferiority to the end of their days.

The other major factor, as he saw it, was on a more physical plane. Had I realised, he asked, that during all those years none of us had seen, heard, touched or been touched by a woman? I assured him that this fact had not passed me by unnoticed, and went on to tell him of my appendix operation, and how I had been tended by a nun for two days in 1942, but he dismissed it out of hand. "Nuns don't count," he said firmly. Had I realised, he continued, that we had been in close proximity to fellow officers the whole time? I assured him that I hadn't failed to observe that either. He went on to explain some of the likely effects of this long-term deprivation of women, more especially at that particular period in our young lives when everything would normally have been so different. He made it very clear, however, that he didn't think we were all likely to go 'peculiar', as he put it, but he did enlarge on what he considered the effects might be. It was at this point that he harked back to remind me of someone else we both knew; had I heard that this man had been laid low with devastating headaches since his return home and that there seemed to be no end to them? This time I couldn't help but be intrigued, if only to find out what the cure might be. Apparently there was no cure, other than consulting a psychiatrist, who should be able to help. I had the feeling that this was just what I was doing though without premeditation, appointment or even fee!

Anxious not to end our conversation on the less happy aspects of our recent life, I looked for some indication from him that there were at least some beneficial effects as well. The ensuing discussion was decidedly more cheerful, and on parting company I felt very grateful for this chance meeting.

During the remainder of my leave, much time must have been devoted to further reflection, and the more I came to learn about what had happened in Europe during the war the more it dawned on me how incredibly lucky I was to be alive at all.

Although clearly and wholly irrational, there is a widely held belief that illness, accidents and disasters are things that happen only to other people. I had heard of, and even witnessed some of, the appalling atrocities that had taken place, but somehow such things had always happened to others. One such example, which had only recently come to light, concerned some forty officers who, towards the end of the war, had escaped, but were recaptured and rounded up. Herded into two trucks, they were being taken – as they were led to believe – back to their camp. On the way they were given a short break in a field and while they were standing around together, their guards suddenly opened fire on them with their automatic weapons, gunning them all down where they stood.

"War reveals dimensions of human nature both above and below the acceptable standards of humanity." So wrote J. Glenn Gray in his book '*The Warriors – Reflections on Men in Battle*'. Most of the dimensions I encountered in Germany were those that fell below the lower standards of humanity. In the years that followed the war so many horrors came to be revealed that believing that such barbarous savagery could have been perpetrated by any so-called civilised being against another – even in war time – went almost beyond the realm of human understanding. Yet there was any amount of evidence to prove that what had happened was beyond all doubt true. By comparison, we, being for the most part spared from such brutality, had only to learn how to come to terms with captivity itself and, indeed, how to survive it.

Final Army Service

As my long leave was coming to an end a summons arrived for me to attend an interview at the War Office. I had already learnt through meeting several others in a similar situation to myself that we had each been allotted a number, its significance being that if it was 25 or over the holder was destined to undergo re-training for the war against Japan. I had been given the number 24. Whilst the prospect of having to attend courses and start military training once again was hardly attractive, to have been marked down as not worthy of further training didn't do much to restore any degree of self-confidence. Some friends who had already been interviewed disclosed to me the sort of dead-end jobs that were on offer, and warned me about one in particular – a warning for which I was to be very grateful.

"Remind me," asked the interviewing officer, "what stage of military training had you reached before you were taken prisoner?" I might just well have answered that I could cope with bows and arrows. He gave me a wan smile, sighed one of those 'I'm trying to be as patient as I can' sighs, and told me there was a vacancy for an ADRTO in one of the main stations in Birmingham. One of the drawbacks of being out of England for so long was that most people, particular in the services, now referred to almost everything by its initials, and I had no idea what they stood for. I did, however, have a strong feeling that I didn't want to be posted to Birmingham. My querying the initials triggered off another sigh, and I was informed that they stood for Assistant Deputy Railway Transport Officer. Seeing at once that this had no appeal, my interviewer tried again: "How about RTO at Aberystwyth?" He really needn't have asked. I had spotted what RTO stood for, and the thought of pacing up and down the platform of a station on the Welsh coast was even less attractive. "Would there be any other opportunities?" I ventured. He ruffled through a file and came up with the offer of my joining some Commission to do with reparations, which could mean going back to Germany. The thought of returning to that country in a position of authority, over those who had lorded it over us for so long, sparked but a momentary show of enthusiasm, which was extinguished as quickly as it had arisen. Common sense prevailed; no way did I seriously want to go back to Germany – ever.

Brightening up, my interviewer presented another suggestion. His tone this time indicated that this was the special one that he had been keeping up his sleeve and it would therefore be welcomed with gratitude. "SSVs!" he announced with an air of finality. This stood for Short Sea Voyages, and was the one posting about which I had been warned. It involved being Ship's Adjutant on a cross-Channel steamer, making the journey two or three times a day in all weathers. I had heard of one officer, whose name was vaguely familiar to me, who had unthinkingly accepted this post only to find himself (he was a poor sailor) throwing up into the Channel several times a week, and oblivious most of the time of the still present danger of floating mines. My aversion to this offer must have been plain enough. It was greeted with a hopeless shrug of the shoulders, and was followed by what really was the final suggestion: "I don't suppose that LSVs would find much favour either. Very few of those returning from years overseas seem at all keen to go…" But I didn't need to listen any more. I had realised at once that this meant Long Sea Voyages and I couldn't imagine anything better. It may not have been quite what Hippocrates had had in mind but it wasn't all that far off his great idea for the healing of minds and bodies on the island of Cos.

"You realise, do you," he went on, "that acceptance of this appointment may well involve you being away for months at a time, and that it may include extended travel to Australia or New Zealand?" I just knew that this was for me, and to my interviewer's immense surprise, and obvious relief, I thanked him profusely and left with the promise of an early promotion to Captain.

On 6th August, and after extensive warnings, the first atomic bomb was dropped on Japan, followed by a second three days later. These two bombs caused horrific and widespread destruction of the towns of Hiroshima and Nagasaki. Such total devastation and appalling havoc was beyond anyone's experience or even imagination, and it was hardly surprising that it led some of the very few survivors to believe that they were witnessing the end of the world.

Well before the dropping of these bombs Japan was already

doomed. Allied maritime power dominated what was left of the Japanese Navy and had already secured vital ocean bases from which the final assault on her armies could be mounted. The effect of the atomic bombs was such that no further military action was necessary as within a few days Japan agreed to the Allied Powers' terms of surrender, the announcement of which was made in Britain by the newly elected Prime Minister – Clement Attlee – on 14th August.

Such was the stupendous impact of the dramatic display of atomic power that one leading newspaper of the day abandoned referring to time in terms of Anno Domini in favour of 'Day One of the Atomic Era'. Day Two, Three and so on continued for some months before, without any further comment, the idea was suddenly dropped.

These earth-shattering events took place during the last few weeks of my leave and I shared the general feeling of enormous relief that the war against Japan was now over and that all fighting had now ceased; and yet there was also a deep anxiety about the enormous power of this terrifying new weapon, coupled with grave misgivings about when and where it might ever be used again. Nearly sixty years after the dropping of these bombs, sadly, very little has happened to reduce such apprehension.

Any further thoughts on this depressing subject were soon dispelled by the welcome news that my promotion had come through, and, as Ship's Adjutant on the SS Franconia, I was soon on my way to Bombay. Under the authority of a Colonel and a

Cunard White Star SS "Franconia."

Major I quickly found that the posting carried considerable respon-sibility. This, at last was something very welcome indeed, and it led to a growing return of self-confidence. It was just great to be doing something positive after so long a period of inactivity.

There was little time to see anything of Bombay because the stay there was very brief. In fact the embarkation of several army units took place within less than two days after our arrival. Amongst these units and a number of civilians, were fifteen soldiers who had been prisoners of the Japanese. I was expecting to see emaciated men; but not so. They were mostly in good physical shape, having been freed some weeks previously, and I was most anxious to meet them. Their first thought was how dreadful it must have been for us in Germany because we hadn't been made to work as they had, and so what on earth had we done with our time all day? During the voyage back to Liverpool I learnt a great deal about life, and rather more about death, in Japanese hands, and was ever more thankful that it had been my lot to have been in Germany.

After a short leave I was once again on my way; this time on the SS Orion to Australia and New Zealand. It was unfortunate that what was to have been my first Christmas at home for six years was actually to be spent on this troubled vessel. Troubled it certainly was, mainly because, for some inexplicable reason, the departure date arranged for its voyage to Malta with two regiments on board was Christmas Eve. The plight of the men involved was highlighted with special emphasis in the tabloid press, and questions were asked in Parliament about who had ordered this departure for such an insensitive time. Feelings ran high enough for the makings of a riot on board, this only being averted by orders hastily being given for departure a few hours before schedule. That night at sea, as we were on our southerly route from Liverpool, I listened to the BBC Nine o'clock News, the first item on which reported the story of the SS Orion's unhappy sailing that day. Any anxiety about continuing trouble on board was soon dispelled as we headed into a severe gale in the Bay of Biscay, where I spent the most wretched Christmas ever. But good cheer for the troops was on its way – or was it?

The press had demanded to know what provision had been made for the troops to celebrate Christmas. Clearly questions would be asked in high places, so hundreds of cases of bottled beer had been loaded on board. My instructions couldn't have been made clearer: no way was there to be even a hint of complaint about any lack of Christmas cheer; I was to ensure that my team would see to it that every single man on board was given his two bottles "whether he wants them or not!"

Feeling distinctly queasy myself – the ship had no stabilisers – and with many of those detailed to distribute the bottles laid low themselves by sea-sickness, I somehow managed to start the operation. With mountainous waves all around, the very sight of which only generated an increasing unease in a stomach already severely tested, I urged the stalwarts in my depleted team to thrust two bottles into the hands of each and every soldier. It was amazing how far the ship could roll without turning right over, and this rolling, together with the pronounced pitching motion and the crashing of enormous waves, made a mere glance at even one bottle enough to cause several of the soldiers to throw up on the spot. In spite of this we went resolutely on for most of that morning. Quite early on, however, we did drop the "Happy Christmas!" which we were supposed to wish them all, mainly because it sounded increasingly hollow but also because of the many unprintable answers we received. The ghastly voyage ended two days later in the Maltese port of Valletta, where the troops almost fell over each other in their anxiety to step onto dry land.

A day later the SS Orion called at Taranto in the heel of Italy, the port of embarkation for the Second New Zealand Expeditionary Force, whose members just about filled all available accommodation. It became clear at once that there was no need for any British staff to run the ship, and so for the next three or four weeks all we had to do was sit back and enjoy the rest of the voyage.

Calling first for a day in the South Island, at Christchurch, the SS Orion went on to stay for ten days at Wellington, in the North Island, giving me an opportunity to enjoy a wonderful tour of the country. In addition, on the way home there was another unscheduled stop for five days in South Australia. These very welcome breaks were made all the more enjoyable because they were totally unexpected.

The whole voyage lasted about three months and it proved to be enormously beneficial, doing a great deal to restore health in body and mind. The sun, the sea air and the stimulation of extensive travel, coupled with a responsible job, all combined to create a very much happier outlook on life. There couldn't have been a better way in which to finish the long period of active service.

So ended, from September 1939 to April 1946, just over six and a half years of military service.

Reflections on Captivity

From the moment he is sentenced, the convicted prisoner can calculate his probable date of release. The prisoner-of-war, however, has no knowing how long he will remain captive, nor does he even know for certain that he will eventually return to his homeland at all. Very few, if any, in the Great War of 1914-1918 remained a prisoner for longer than four years, but in the Second World War it was just possible for some – mainly RAF – to have been captive for longer than the four years and eleven months period that was the lot of those unable to make it home from Dunkirk in May, 1940.

In spite of the continuous uncertainty about how long captivity might last, I have never looked upon the years spent in Germany as wasted; wasted youth in some respects, perhaps, but not altogether so. While it was hardly an experience anyone would choose for himself, in a totally unexpected way it compensated to some extent for the lack of a university education.

The undoubted advantages of a further education for three years or so within the dignified precincts of some eminent seat of learning had sadly passed me by. However, a rather longer period within the inglorious boundaries of barbed wire generated at least an opportunity for another kind of education, far less academic but no less real; in many ways much more so. It began almost immediately after the initial shock of sudden captivity. Gradually it became increasingly clear that confinement for however long is not to be set aside as some grim slice *out of* life but, rather, it is a slice of life itself. Education by experience hadn't suddenly stopped; it had, in fact, increased, and most of what could be learnt that would be of lasting value came that way rather than from study. Some such experiences were extremely unpleasant; yet there were others that were both gracious and uplifting.

During the first few months time hung heavily, but then after a while it could be seen as something precious – something not to be wasted. It became clear that opportunities existed to develop talents already possessed, and maybe to acquire others as yet unconsidered. I could never have imagined, for instance, that forgery, which had had a practical purpose at the time, would ever be on my list of skills to be learnt and practised. There were many other, rather more edifying, subjects in the realms of art, literature and music, which could be studied by minds still highly active and capable of development. It was, perhaps, enlightening for the young, as so many of us were, to discover that what they did, did not have to be useful to be valuable.

It was extraordinary, at the time anyway, how some normally insignificant factor could bring colour to a drab situation. An unexpected morsel of food, the chance acquisition of a slightly less hard straw pillow, or even just observing the beauty of a starry sky were enough to lead to the conviction that this new life of captivity was indeed something in itself. When a life is suddenly shattered by bereavement or a serious accident, there comes a time soon afterwards when the same life has to be rebuilt, but on very different, less familiar and probably less pleasing foundations. This is precisely the situation of the newly captured; and the first step in this new direction was to realise that, even though hemmed in behind barbed wire and locked doors it was possible that windows might be opening.

The sameness of prison life could become almost intolerable, until the day of discovery that there existed a variety within oneself; a realisation that could lead to an extraordinary peace in mind and body. This surprising tranquillity wouldn't last for very long, but from time to time it could be brought back; none too easily amidst the noise and company of many others, but nevertheless possible, even though there was hardly a minute in any day in which to be entirely alone. It was never my lot to be sentenced to any time in solitary confinement, which was a punishment reserved for those caught, or on occasions even suspected of, breaking camp rules. Those who did have a brief spell in the 'cooler' certainly wouldn't have liked it to have lasted for too long, but were not at all unhappy with their few days of utter peace and quiet; some even said that they had almost forgotten what it was like to be still.

One of the abiding impressions of prisoner-of-war life that remains with me is not so much sympathy but an empathy with prisoners anywhere. Although their varied circumstances and mine might well be vastly different, we should have suffered the one vital factor common to us all – the loss of personal liberty coupled with the humiliating and total dependence on others. I am reminded of this from time to time, especially when we are asked in church to pray for all prisoners and captives.

This utter dependence on others was brought home to us each and every day by the provision of food, however meagre, by the enemy, as well as by the very welcome supplies sent from Britain. We were ever on the receiving end of everything we needed, especially food and clothing. In our earlier lives most of us would have had a fair idea how to acquire for ourselves what we wanted, but since childhood scant attention would have been paid to how to receive. If not wholly aware of the sacrifices and difficulties our families were experiencing in sending us anything at all, we could at least imagine them and that in itself gave rise to an uneasiness that was made worse by our very limited ability, at least until after the war, to express any kind of real gratitude.

The fighting that we were involved in for so brief a period is long since over. The dust has settled and the whole war experience now been consigned to whatever historical filing department the brain may provide for such purpose. Too much introspection cannot be good for anyone, and I find that all reflections on the war years have now virtually ceased. My only regret is not having been given any opportunity to take part in the destruction of the armies of evil that had caused so much misery to so many throughout Europe.

One final reflection, however, is worthy of inclusion and it is all to do with exercising patience; hardly a practice that had formed part of any military training programme, and for the young hardly considered at all. To live closely, all too closely, with other men for a long time develops a degree of patience that is so vital to any kind of harmony. I have a feeling that any monk would say the same, but unlike life in a monastery where the emphasis is on the spiritual, we found ourselves on the lower plane of a very worldly life in which personal survival was the chief factor. This in turn meant depending on friends, and I cannot think of any more abiding lesson from all those years than that of learning the true value of friends – especially in adversity. Yet even the closest friendships have their limitations; bounds which instinctively are not crossed so as not to risk stretching the relationship beyond breaking point.

There were occasions when it could have been a wonderful relief to talk rather than just write to family, but it could not be. A number of us were, I believe, thus drawn to the rather obvious conclusion that the centre of our lives was our own soul and always had been, and that as a prisoners we were perforce driven in upon ourselves more than we might have been if we had been free. Consciously or not, we all came to acquire varying degrees of patience and perhaps to realise that it is not a passive virtue. There is nothing of the lethargic or laid back in the words of Milton's finest sonnet, when he wrote: "They also serve who only stand and wait." Stand, he said, not lounge about; and wait – wait alert and prepared for a call to action, knowing that it may never come.

Appendix

Serial No. 8158 .... *Belson* .... Army Form B 108D.

Certificate of discharge from (a) *Territorial Army*

No. 859915 .... Rank *Gunner*

Name BELSON *Dorrien Berkeley Ewan*
(Surname) (Christian names in full)

Corps from which discharged } *Royal Artillery*

Also served during this engagement in.....................

N.B.—The following particulars refer only to the engagement from which the man is now being discharged :—

Enlisted at *Putney* on 14 9 1936

(b)

Medals, Clasps, Decorations, Mentions in Despatches. Any special acts of gallantry or distinguished conduct brought to notice in brigade or superior orders.

Discharged ~~in consequence of~~ *At his own request*
(Para 204 (3) T. A. Regs)

AFTER HAVING SERVED :—

~~(c) with the Colours (h)~~ .... years.
.... days.

~~(d) in Section " B " ARMY RESERVE (h)~~ .... years.
.... days.

~~(e) in Section " D " ARMY RESERVE (h)~~
~~(f) in the SUPPLEMENTARY RESERVE~~ } (h) ONE years.
(g) in the TERRITORIAL ARMY (h) 295 days.

Date of discharge 5 . 7 . 38

Description of the above-named man on Enlistment :—

Year of birth 1917 .... Marks or Scars.....................

Height 6 ft. 3 ins.

Complexion *Dark*

Eyes *Blue* Hair *Dark*

Place *Woolwich* ....Signature and Rank *R.A*

Date 11 . 7 . 38 Officer i/c Records.

Special Attention is directed to the Notes on reverse. C.D. ⋆ A.A.

(*2268) Wt.21753/1723 50,000 (6 up) 8/37 A.&E.W.Ltd. Gp.698 Forms/B108D/9 [P.T.O.

DORRIEN Berkeley BELSON re-enlisted in T.A. (ARTISTS RIFLES) on 2nd MAY. 1939

Territorial Army Record

141

163 O.C.T.U./406

Certificate of Transfer or Re-transfer to the Army Reserve, Discharge or Disembodiment.

This Certificate will be used in the following cases :—

(i) Re-transfer to the Army Reserve or discharge in the case of a Mobilized Section "A" or "B" Army Reservist, or a Section "D" Reservist who re-engaged into that Section direct from the Colours or from Section "B" Army Reserve.

(ii) Transfer to the Army Reserve or discharge in the case of a Mobilized Section "D" Army Reservist enlisted direct into that section or a Mobilized Supplementary Reservist ; or

(iii) Disembodiment or discharge in the case of a man of the embodied Territorial Army.

N.B.—All words which are inapplicable to be struck out.

(a) Army Number _859915._

(b) Name _BELSON._ _Dorrien Berkeley Evan_ .
(Surname.) (Christian Names in full.)

(c) Date of joining or re-joining the Colours (on mobilization or embodiment). _2 - 9 - 39._

(d) Date of ~~transfer or re-transfer to the Army Reserve~~; discharge ~~or disembodiment~~. _16 - 12 - 39._

(e) Service with the Colours _—_ years _106_ days.

Service not with the Colours _—_ years _—_ days.

Total Service _—_ years _229._ days.

(f) Rank on ~~transfer, re-transfer~~, discharge ~~or disembodiment~~. _Cadet._

(g) Cause of ~~transfer, re-transfer~~, discharge ~~or disembodiment~~. _Apptd to a Commission in Gloucester Regt 2-9- dated 19-12-39._

(h) Corps from which ~~transferred~~, re-transferred, discharged ~~or disembodied~~. _163rd O.C.T.U. Artists Rifles._

(j) Campaigns, including actions (i)

(k) Medals, Clasps, Decorations, Mentions in Despatches. Any special acts of gallantry or distinguished conduct brought to notice in brigade or superior orders (ii). (i)

O'Dowr. Colonel Signature and Rank.

Officer i/c _Kyle_ Records.

Date _7 - 2 - 40_ Place _Winchester._

NOTES :—

(i) This portion to be struck out if no entry is required.
(ii) If there is not sufficient room for the insertion here of the record of any special act of gallantry or distinguished conduct, such record will be written on the reverse of the Army Form and signed by the Officer who attests the certificate, and a reference made here to such entry.

See overleaf for description of above-named man on Transfer, or Re-transfer to the Army Reserve, Discharge or Disembodiment, and assessments of Conduct and Character.

IF THIS CERTIFICATE IS LOST NO DUPLICATE CAN BE OBTAINED.

Army Transfer Certificate

Disease such as meningitis claimed the life of a fellow officer.

Prisoner of war theatrical performances kept up morale in the camp.

Bibliography

The Quill, by Captain E.G.C. Beckwith, TD. Country Life Limited, 2 Tavistock Street, Covent Garden, London. First published 1947.

Joe in Germany, by Jimmy Graham and Jack Thomas, printed by The Surrey Fine Art Press, Redhill, Surrey, 1946.

The Egoist, by George Meredith. Oxford University Press, 1879. Also, World's Classics edition.

Massacre on the Road to Dunkirk. Wormhout 1940, by Leslie Aitken, MBE. Patrick Stephens Ltd, 2nd edition, 1988.

Ena, Spain's English Queen, by Gerard Noel, Constable & Co Ltd, London, 2000.

The Second World War, Volume 1, *The Gathering Storm*, by Winston S Churchill, Cassell & Co Ltd, 1948.

The Warriors – Reflections on Men in Battle, by J Glenn Gray.

Extracts from War Diary of 5th Bn. (T.A.) January–May 1940, by Major F.W Priestley, provided by Major (Rt'd) CPT Rebbeck.

On Being a Prisoner, pamphlet produced by the European Student Relief Fund, Geneva 1943. Some material formerly reproduced in *The Times Literary Supplement*.

Selected Poems 1908–1956, by Siegfried Sassoon, Faber & Faber, London, 1968.